Writing with POWER

Language Skills Practice
Grammar, Usage, and Mechanics

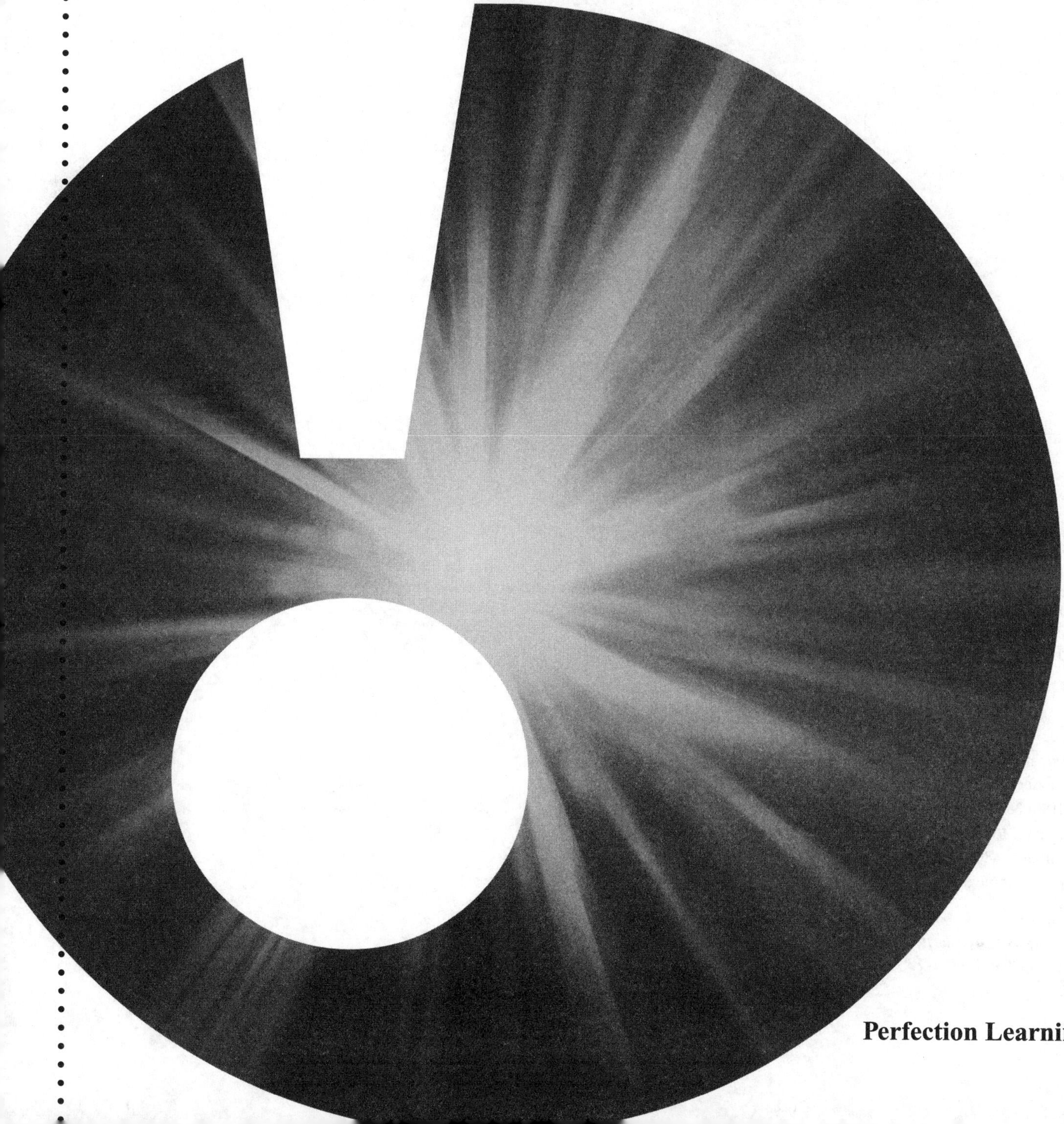

Perfection Learning®

© 2011 Perfection Learning® Corporation

The purchase of this book entitles an individual teacher to reproduce pages for use in the classroom. This permitted use of copyrighted material does not extend beyond the building level. Reproduction for use in an entire school system or for commercial use is prohibited. Beyond the classroom use by an individual teacher, reproduction, transmittal, or retrieval of this work is prohibited without written permission from the publisher.

Printed in the United States of America.

1 2 3 4 5 6 WC 16 15 14 13 12 11

For information, contact
Perfection Learning® Corporation
1000 North Second Avenue, P.O. Box 500
Logan, Iowa 51546-0500
Phone: 1-800-831-4190 • Fax: 1-800-543-2745
perfectionlearning.com

77971
ISBN-13: 978-0-7891-7983-8
ISBN-10: 0-7891-7983-0

Table of Contents

Grammar

Chapter 13 The Parts of Speech
Common and Proper Nouns................ 1
Concrete, Abstract, Compound, and
  Collective Nouns 2
Personal Pronouns........................ 3
Reflexive, Intensive, Indefinite, Demonstrative,
  and Interrogative Pronouns........... 4–5
Transitive and Intransitive Verbs.......... 6–7
Verb Phrases 8–9
Linking Verbs 10–11
Adjective, Noun, or Pronoun?............ 12
Proper and Compound Adjectives 13–14
Adverbs............................... 15
Adverbs and Adjectives 16
Prepositions........................ 17–18
Conjunctions.......................... 19
Conjunctions and Interjections 20
Parts of Speech Review 21

Chapter 14 The Sentence Base
Simple Subjects and Predicates 22–23
Different Positions of Subjects 24
Compound Subjects and Compound
  Verbs............................... 25
Sentence Fragments 26
Direct Objects......................... 27
Indirect Objects 28
Direct and Indirect Objects.............. 29
Objective Complements.................. 30
Subject Complements.................... 31
Sentence Patterns 32
Sentence Base Review 33–34

Chapter 15 Phrases
Prepositional Phrases 35–36
Appositives and Appositive Phrases..... 37–38
Punctuation with Appositives and
  Appositive Phrases 39–40
Participles and Participial Phrases....... 41–42
Punctuation with Participial Phrases 43
Gerunds and Gerund Phrases 44–45
Infinitives and Infinitive Phrases........... 46
Participles, Gerunds, and Infinitives........ 47
Misplaced and Dangling Modifiers 48
Phrases Review 49–50

Chapter 16 Clauses
Independent and Subordinate Clauses...... 51
Adverbial Clauses................... 52–53
Punctuation with Adverbial Clauses 54
Elliptical Clauses....................... 55
Adjectival Clauses 56
Relative Pronouns in Adjectival Clauses..... 57
Punctuation with Adjectival Clauses 58
Misplaced Modifiers 59
Noun Clauses...................... 60–61
Adverbial, Adjectival, and Noun Clauses 62
Kinds of Sentence Structure.............. 63
Clause Fragments...................... 64
Run-on Sentences 65
Fragments and Run-on Sentences 66
Clauses Review 67

Usage

Chapter 17 Using Verbs
Principal Parts of Irregular Verbs 68–70
Verb Tense....................... 71–72
Uses of the Tenses 73–74
Progressive and Emphatic Forms 75
Shifts in Tense......................... 76
Using Correct Verb Forms 77
Active and Passive Voice 78
Mood................................ 79
Using Verbs Review..................... 80

Chapter 18 Using Pronouns
The Nominative Case of Pronouns....... 81–82
The Objective Case of Pronouns 83–84
The Possessive Case of Pronouns 85
Nominative, Objective, and Possessive Case
  Pronouns 86
Who and *Whom* in Clauses................ 87
Pronouns in Elliptical Clauses.............. 88
Pronouns and Their Antecedents........... 89
Indefinite Pronouns as Antecedents 90
Unclear, Missing, or Confusing
  Antecedents 91
Using Pronouns Review.................. 92

continued

Table of Contents *continued*

Chapter 19 Subject and Verb Agreement
Agreement of Subjects and Verbs 93
Agreement and Interrupting Words 94
Compound Subjects 95–96
Indefinite Pronouns as Subjects 97
Subjects in Inverted Order 98
Other Agreement Problems.......... 99–100
Subject and Verb Agreement Review 101

Chapter 20 Using Adjectives and Adverbs
Regular Comparisons 102–103
Irregular Comparisons 104–105
Problems with Comparisons......... 106–107
Problems with Modifiers................. 108
Double Negatives 109
Using Adjectives and Adverbs Review...... 110

Mechanics

Chapter 21 Capital Letters
Capitalizing Proper Nouns 111–112
Capitalizing Proper Adjectives....... 113–114
Capitalizing Titles 115–116
Capitalization Review.................... 117

Chapter 22 End Marks and Commas
End Marks 118
Periods with Abbreviations 119
Commas That Separate 120–121
Commas in Compound Sentences 122–123
Commas After Introductory
    Elements 124–125
Commonly Used Commas 126
Commas with Appositives, Adjectives,
    Titles, and Degrees............ 127–128
Commas with Nonessential Elements 129
End Marks and Commas Review.......... 130

Chapter 23 Other Punctuation
The Possessive Form of Nouns........ 131–132
The Possessive Form of Pronouns..... 133–134
Apostrophes and Joint Ownership......... 135
Other Uses of Apostrophes................ 136
Semicolons Between Clauses; with
    Transitional Words 137
Semicolons to Avoid Confusion........... 138
Colons 139
Italics (Underlining)..................... 140
Quotation Marks with Titles 141
Direct Quotations 142
Commas and End Marks with Direct
    Quotations 143
Hyphens 144
Dashes and Parentheses 145
Other Punctuation Review 146

Chapter 24 Spelling
Spelling Patterns 147–148
Plurals 149–150
Spelling Numbers....................... 151
Prefixes and Suffixes................ 152–153
Spelling Review 154

Appendix
Power Rules...................... 155–158
Power Rules Review 159

Name _____ Date _____

CHAPTER 13 — Common and Proper Nouns

[13A.2] Common nouns name any person, place, or thing. **Proper nouns** name a particular person, place, or thing.

> **EXERCISE A** Write C if the underlined word or group of words is a common noun or P if it is a proper noun.

_____ 1. The Virgin Islands National Park on the island of <u>St. John's</u> is an unusual park.

_____ 2. This park is partly under <u>water.</u>

_____ 3. People use <u>snorkels</u> or scuba gear in the park.

_____ 4. Clear underwater trails lead to coral <u>forests</u>.

_____ 5. Visitors see octopuses, tropical <u>fish</u>, and turtles.

_____ 6. Underwater parks are located in various <u>parts</u> of the world.

_____ 7. One such park is the <u>John Pennekamp Coral Reef State Park</u>.

_____ 8. This attraction is located near <u>Key Largo</u> in Florida.

_____ 9. The visitor there finds a <u>fairyland</u> of undersea life.

_____ 10. Many types of plants and <u>coral</u> grow there.

_____ 11. <u>Visitors</u> can learn much about undersea life in Florida.

_____ 12. Another popular attraction is <u>Dry Tortugas National Park</u> in Key West.

_____ 13. The Dry Tortugas are seven <u>islands</u> that were formed from sand and coral reefs.

_____ 14. <u>Juan Ponce de León</u> set foot on the Dry Tortugas in 1513.

_____ 15. The islands were named after the <u>turtles</u> he found there.

Name _____ Date _____

CHAPTER 13 Concrete, Abstract, Compound, and Collective Nouns

[13A.1] Concrete nouns name people, places, or things. **Abstract nouns** name ideas and qualities.
[13A.3] Compound nouns are nouns that include more than one word.
[13A.4] Collective nouns name a group of people or things.

EXERCISE A Choose whether each underlined noun is concrete, abstract, compound, or collective.

_____ 1. The colony of honeybees was endangered by pesticides.
    A compound
    B collective

_____ 2. The baby cried with disappointment when he spilled his ice cream.
    A concrete
    B abstract

_____ 3. The team members jumped up and down after their big win.
    A collective
    B compound

_____ 4. Mrs. Erwin wished to donate money to a good cause.
    A concrete
    B abstract

_____ 5. David's brother sipped soda through a silly straw.
    A concrete
    B abstract

_____ 6. The businessmen ignored the old man's refusal.
    A concrete
    B abstract

_____ 7. Which type of butterfly migrates to Mexico every fall?
    A compound
    B collective

EXERCISE B Underline all of the concrete, abstract, compound, and collective nouns in the following sentences. Write the kind of noun above each one.

8. The concept of democracy is an old one.

9. The class had a secret plan.

10. Walt Disney's films often deal with fantasy.

11. The flock of crows was very noisy.

12. The rainbow stretched across the morning sky.

13. The dedication of many research scientists is amazing.

Name _____ Date _____

CHAPTER 13 Personal Pronouns

[13B] A **pronoun** is a word that takes the place of one or more nouns.

[13B.1] Personal pronouns are the most common kind of pronoun and can be divided into three groups: first person, second person, and third person.

> **EXERCISE A** Underline the personal pronoun(s) in each sentence. Then draw an arrow to the antecedent(s) of the underlined pronoun.

1. Jack asked Marisa if she had seen his missing dog.

2. Heidi asked the furniture repairer, "Please take a look at my bureau against that wall."

3. Tina, where have you put your pocketbook?

4. The girls said that they were practicing their piano duet.

5. "Is this glass of cider yours or mine?" Dennis asked Louisa.

6. Did Rita take the present and hide it somewhere?

7. Does Billy own his own car or motorbike?

8. "We are going to the football game," announced Sandra and Dee.

> **EXERCISE B** Rewrite each sentence, replacing unnecessary nouns with pronouns.

9. "Will Robin meet Beth at the theater?" Sherry asked Beth.
   _____

10. Clifford asked Ginni if Ginni had a spare pen.
    _____

11. The visitors said that several of the visitors had seen the play.
    _____
    _____

12. "If this radio is Harry's, where is Nick's?" Nick asked Clarence.
    _____
    _____

Name _____ Date _____

CHAPTER 13 — Reflexive, Intensive, Indefinite, Demonstrative, and Interrogative Pronouns

[13B.2] A **reflexive pronoun** refers to the noun or the pronoun that is the subject of the sentence. It is needed to make the meaning of the sentence clear.

[13B.4] **Indefinite pronouns** often refer to unnamed people or things.

[13B.5] A **demonstrative pronoun** is used to point out a specific person, place, or object.

[13B.6] An **interrogative pronoun** is used to ask a question.

> **EXERCISE** Identify whether the underlined pronouns are reflexive, intensive, indefinite, demonstrative, or interrogative.

_____ 1. <u>Both</u> have political strengths and shortcomings.
  A reflexive
  B intensive
  C indefinite
  D demonstrative
  E interrogative

_____ 2. The candidates <u>themselves</u> do not seem to think highly of each other.
  A reflexive
  B intensive
  C indefinite
  D demonstrative
  E interrogative

_____ 3. I cannot decide between <u>either</u> of the two.
  A reflexive
  B intensive
  C indefinite
  D demonstrative
  E interrogative

_____ 4. Do you really want to order <u>those</u>?
  A reflexive
  B intensive
  C indefinite
  D demonstrative
  E interrogative

_____ 5. <u>Which</u> of these belong to you?
  A reflexive
  B intensive
  C indefinite
  D demonstrative
  E interrogative

_____ 6. <u>This</u> is the last thing I need to do today.
  A reflexive
  B intensive
  C indefinite
  D demonstrative
  E interrogative

_____ 7. Will you give <u>these</u> to your friend?
  A reflexive
  B intensive
  C indefinite
  D demonstrative
  E interrogative

_____ 8. <u>Who</u> took my pen?
  A reflexive
  B intensive
  C indefinite
  D demonstrative
  E interrogative

_____ 9. Did Brea Anne make <u>herself</u> a hot cup of tea?
  A reflexive
  B intensive
  C indefinite
  D demonstrative
  E interrogative

CHAPTER 13 Reflexive, Intensive, Indefinite, Demonstrative, and Interrogative Pronouns

EXERCISE Underline the pronoun in each sentence. Then label it as *reflexive, intensive, indefinite, demonstrative,* or *interrogative*.

_____ 1. The President himself gives many political speeches.

_____ 2. Our representatives must get themselves elected.

_____ 3. Who is our state representative?

_____ 4. Someone must take charge of a campaign.

_____ 5. A candidate usually hires herself a manager.

_____ 6. The manager himself does not usually give campaign speeches.

_____ 7. Those funds are set aside for the campaign.

_____ 8. Few can afford the expense of a campaign otherwise.

_____ 9. Many run for the same office.

_____ 10. What are the qualifications for office?

_____ 11. We ourselves must decide on the best candidate.

_____ 12. That certainly wasn't the right voting place.

_____ 13. My sister will give herself some time off from work to vote.

_____ 14. Who has been following the elections?

_____ 15. These are the sample ballots for the election.

Name _____ Date _____

CHAPTER 13 — Transitive and Intransitive Verbs

[13C.2] An action verb that has an object is **transitive**. An action verb that has no object is **intransitive**.

EXERCISE A Choose whether the underlined verb in each sentence is transitive (T) or intransitive (I).

_____ 1. Lightning <u>hits</u> more often than you would think.

_____ 2. Lightning <u>occurs</u> even when it is not raining outside.

_____ 3. Each year lightning <u>injures</u> many people in the United States.

_____ 4. Lightning also <u>destroys</u> buildings and other property.

_____ 5. In addition it <u>causes</u> approximately 7,000 forest fires each year.

_____ 6. Lightning <u>strikes</u> with a crack and a flash.

_____ 7. It sometimes <u>uproots</u> full-grown trees in its path.

_____ 8. Loud or frequent thunder <u>indicates</u> approaching lightning activity.

EXERCISE B Underline the action verb in each sentence. Then label it T for transitive or I for intransitive in the blank provided.

_____ 9. These rods conduct lightning into water or the ground.

_____ 10. The rods rest on the roofs of buildings.

_____ 11. Lightning provides a brilliant electrical display.

_____ 12. It actually helps many farmers and gardeners.

_____ 13. Nitrogen composes eighty percent of our air.

_____ 14. Plants need nitrogen as food.

_____ 15. Nitrogen undergoes chemical changes during a lightning storm.

_____ 16. These changes free nitrogen for plant use.

CHAPTER 13 — Transitive and Intransitive Verbs

EXERCISE Choose whether the underlined verbs in the following paragraph are transitive or intransitive. Write T for transitive or I for intransitive in the blanks provided.

Hailstorms are a normal occurrence in much of the United States. We **(1)** <u>expect</u> them during the summer especially. Southern states like Texas, Nebraska, and Oklahoma most frequently **(2)** <u>experience</u> hail. Hailstorms **(3)** <u>cause</u> much damage to houses and automobiles. They **(4)** <u>blast</u> windows and damage roofs every year. Hailstorms in populated areas **(5)** <u>bring</u> dangerous driving conditions. Hail also **(6)** <u>damages</u> farmers' crops. Softball-sized hailstones **(7)** <u>have been produced</u> by some storms. One record-breaking storm **(8)** <u>left</u> a chunk of ice the size of a soccer ball! Large stones **(9)** <u>can fall</u> at speeds over 100 miles per hour. Pebbles, leaves, twigs, and bugs **(10)** <u>have been found</u> in hailstones. However, some soft hailstones **(11)** <u>disintegrate</u> before contact.

1. ____

2. ____

3. ____

4. ____

5. ____

6. ____

7. ____

8. ____

9. ____

10. ____

11. ____

Name _____ Date _____

CHAPTER 13 — Verb Phrases

[13C.3] A **verb phrase** is a main verb plus one or more helping verbs.

EXERCISE Choose the correct verb phrase for each sentence.

_____ 1. All cars must have license plates.
  A must
  B must have

_____ 2. In the old days, license plates were made of leather or wood.
  A were made
  B were made of

_____ 3. A number was stamped on these homemade plates.
  A stamped
  B was stamped

_____ 4. The plate could be attached to any part of the car.
  A could be
  B could be attached

_____ 5. The plate size did vary from state to state.
  A did vary
  B vary

_____ 6. Car manufacturers did not know the size of plates ahead of time.
  A did know
  B did not know

_____ 7. Finally all states did agree on a six-by-twelve-inch plate.
  A did agree
  B did agree on

_____ 8. Many years ago all plates were changed on New Year's Day.
  A were changed
  B were changed on

_____ 9. Today the same plate can be used year after year.
  A can be
  B can be used

_____ 10. A small sticker with a date on it is stuck onto the old plate.
  A stuck
  B is stuck

_____ 11. At one time one plate was required in front and one in back.
  A was required
  B required

_____ 12. Now many states do not use two plates.
  A do use
  B do not use

_____ 13. Many states now are producing specialty plates.
  A now are producing
  B are producing

_____ 14. Mottoes or pictures have been added to those plates.
  A have been
  B have been added

_____ 15. Money from the sale of specialty plates will go to support a state college or a cause.
  A go
  B will go

Name _____ Date _____

CHAPTER 13   Verb Phrases

EXERCISE Underline the verb phrase (main verb plus any helping verbs) in the following sentences.

1. Many license plates in South Dakota <u>do feature</u> logos of various Sioux tribes.

2. Most Wyoming license plates <u>would probably have</u> a picture of a bucking bronco with a rider.

3. This picture <u>was first introduced</u> in 1936.

4. American universities <u>sometimes will offer</u> special license plates to alumni.

5. Most states <u>will issue</u> "vanity" plates that <u>have</u> personal names, initials, or messages on them.

6. There <u>should not be</u> more than eight characters on a license plate, depending on the state.

7. Many "vanity" plates <u>must have been chosen</u> for a humorous effect.

8. For example, a high-speed sports car <u>might have</u> "BCNU" on its license plate.

9. Hobbyists <u>have collected</u> license plates from all over the world.

10. These serious collectors <u>have been collecting</u> license plates for years.

11. Some of the world's oldest license plates <u>were made</u> before 1900.

12. Collectible license plates <u>may be found</u> in auto junkyards.

13. Many collectors <u>will regularly visit</u> scrap yards or rural dumps in search of license plates.

14. Collectors <u>will even go</u> so far as to try to find used plates at the Department of Motor Vehicle offices.

15. The value of a license plate <u>does depend</u> on the plate's condition.

Name _____   Date _____

CHAPTER 13   Linking Verbs

[13C.4] A **linking verb** links the subject with another word in the sentence. The other word either renames or describes the subject.

EXERCISE A Choose the subject and the word that renames or describes it for each sentence.

_____ 1. A hydrofoil is a boat with fins.
    A hydrofoil, boat
    B hydrofoil, fins
    C boat, fins

_____ 2. Dill is one common kind of herb.
    A Dill, herb
    B Dill, one
    C Dill, kind

_____ 3. Tomorrow will be my sister's birthday.
    A Tomorrow, sister's
    B sister's, birthday
    C Tomorrow, birthday

_____ 4. Sonar is an essential aid in the navigation of ships.
    A Sonar, aid
    B navigation, ships
    C Sonar, navigation

_____ 5. The diamond is the birthstone for April.
    A birthstone, April
    B diamond, birthstone
    C diamond, April

_____ 6. The bristlecone pine may be the oldest tree in the world.
    A bristlecone, tree
    B pine, world
    C pine, tree

EXERCISE B Underline the linking verb in each sentence. If a sentence does not have a linking verb, write *none*.

_____ 7. Frank was in the kitchen early this morning.

_____ 8. My geometry and history classes are very difficult this year.

_____ 9. The pilots are recent graduates of the aviation school.

_____ 10. The Long Trail is a footpath across the Green Mountains of Vermont.

_____ 11. The mushrooms are in the back of the refrigerator.

_____ 12. Mexican and East Indian food is often very hot.

_____ 13. Jade may be green, white, or pink.

Name _____ Date _____

CHAPTER 13 Linking Verbs

EXERCISE A Underline the linking verb. Then choose the subject and the word that renames or describes it.

_____ 1. In the night sky, Mars looks red.
  A sky, red
  B night, Mars
  C Mars, red

_____ 2. Francis felt happy about her game.
  A Francis, game
  B Francis, happy
  C happy, game

_____ 3. The climbers grew weary toward the end of the hike.
  A climbers, weary
  B end, hike
  C climbers, end

_____ 4. The clouds turned gray before the storm.
  A clouds, storm
  B gray, storm
  C clouds, gray

_____ 5. Beverly became president of the class after the election.
  A Beverly, class
  B Beverly, president
  C class, election

_____ 6. These roses smell sweet for days after cutting.
  A roses, cutting
  B These, sweet
  C roses, sweet

EXERCISE B Underline the verbs in the following sentences. Then label each one A for action or L for linking. Finally, circle the subject and the word that renames or describes the subject.

_____ 7. The lights appeared dim through the dense fog.

_____ 8. The foliage in their backyard has grown tall.

_____ 9. The whipped cream cake looks absolutely tasty.

_____ 10. The lone adventurer remained in the snake-filled pit.

_____ 11. The cartoon cat's face turned bright green.

_____ 12. That fern feels as soft as a kitten.

_____ 13. The engine of the car doesn't sound healthy.

_____ 14. None of the choices on the menu seems appetizing.

_____ 15. My best friend became a professional dancer.

Name _____   Date _____

CHAPTER 13   Adjective, Noun, or Pronoun?

[13D.1] An **adjective** is a word that modifies a noun or pronoun.
[13A] A **noun** is the name of a person, place, thing, or idea.
[13B] A **pronoun** is a word that takes the place of one or more nouns.

> **EXERCISE** Choose whether the underlined word is an adjective (A), noun (N), or pronoun (P).

_____ 1. A stone lantern is part of many Japanese gardens.

_____ 2. Some cork comes from Spain and Portugal.

_____ 3. The birdbath was hollowed out from a piece of stone.

_____ 4. Silver dollars are rare today.

_____ 5. That Spanish moss has no roots.

_____ 6. Which of these impressive entries will win the prize?

_____ 7. Ron bought a bushel of pink grapefruit and gave me several.

_____ 8. Some of the weeds in these woods are edible.

_____ 9. Cats often eat several meals a day.

_____ 10. That is the only saguaro cactus that is undamaged.

_____ 11. I look forward to the winter because I like to ski.

_____ 12. Silver is a substance used in photography.

_____ 13. A good time for farmers to repair equipment is during the cold winter months.

_____ 14. Cook County is one area of Illinois.

_____ 15. Those are the only boots that are truly waterproof.

_____ 16. The meeting of the officials of the county government will begin at 8:00 p.m.

_____ 17. The camp counselor told a scary story.

_____ 18. That television program was not very interesting.

_____ 19. We arrived at the camp in late afternoon.

_____ 20. Which book should I pick?

Name _____   Date _____

CHAPTER 13 Proper and Compound Adjectives

[13D.2] A **proper adjective** is a special kind of adjective. It is formed from a proper noun and begins with a capital letter.

[13D.3] Compound adjectives are adjectives that are made up of more than one word.

EXERCISE A Underline all the proper adjectives in the following sentences.

1. Seashell jewelry is worn by <u>Polynesian</u> people.

2. Ancient <u>Sumerian</u> goldsmiths used sophisticated gold metalworking techniques.

3. Early <u>Egyptian</u> people wore ivory-studded gems.

4. <u>Native American</u> tribes made turquoise earrings and rawhide necklaces.

5. The early <u>Greek</u> women also wore gemstone articles.

6. <u>Roman</u> soldiers brought gold and semiprecious stones back to Rome after their conquests.

7. Some <u>African</u> people make gold-wire jewelry.

8. Many <u>Roman</u> women used hairpin jewelry.

EXERCISE B Underline all the compound adjectives in the following sentences.

9. The Incas made <u>eye-catching</u> necklaces of gold.

10. Early English jewelers made <u>gem-studded</u> crowns for royalty.

11. Elizabethan nobles wore teardrop pearls as pendants.

12. East Indian women sometimes wear <u>nose-ring</u> jewels.

13. The Balinese women wear handmade headdresses of flowers.

14. Modern Italian jewelers handcraft <u>high-fashion</u> pieces.

15. American manufacturers sometimes make jewelry of <u>human-made</u> materials.

CHAPTER 13 — Proper and Compound Adjectives

EXERCISE Underline the proper or compound adjectives in each sentence.

1. Our young <u>American</u> friend will visit Scotland next semester.
2. The <u>Atlantic</u> cod you bought at the store tastes great.
3. The <u>high-flying</u> team of acrobats won the coveted award.
4. <u>Shakespearean</u> sonnets have been appearing in this particular column of the paper.
5. Juanita has studied the <u>Impressionist</u> style of painting.
6. The <u>Swedish</u> exchange student will stay at our home for three days.
7. Sometimes we ride the busy <u>crosstown</u> bus to get to her house.
8. For such a <u>high-energy</u> toddler, Michael has behaved well today.
9. The garment was described as a <u>wash-and-wear</u> skirt, so I bought it immediately.
10. The <u>Elizabethan</u> garments should be used for tomorrow's costume party.
11. I really wish I could market this clean <u>New Mexican</u> air!
12. Certain people in my novel can be called <u>Dickensian</u> characters.
13. We bought <u>first-class</u> seats for the trip to London.
14. Ralph and Jorge brought their <u>Amazonian</u> python to school today.
15. A <u>sweet-smelling</u> perfume is on sale at the cosmetics counter.
16. Another <u>Olympic</u> swimmer was disqualified today.
17. Many <u>Japanese</u> leaders have met with our country's leaders.
18. The <u>newfangled</u> invention really confused us at first.

Name _____ Date _____

CHAPTER 13 Adverbs

[13D.5] An **adverb** is a word that modifies a verb, an adjective, or another adverb.

EXERCISE A Underline the adverb in each sentence.

1. Flying fish can <u>often</u> soar 1,000 feet at a time.
2. During the summer, storms <u>sometimes</u> occur in the late afternoon.
3. Bread dough <u>usually</u> doubles in size within an hour.
4. Armor <u>once</u> consisted of a helmet, a jacket, and leg covers.
5. The armadillo is a <u>rather</u> unusual animal.
6. That rock star <u>occasionally</u> gives live concerts.
7. <u>Generally</u>, animal sounds convey some meaning to others of the same species.
8. Two <u>fairly</u> recent movies are playing in town this week.
9. The spectators cheered <u>loudly</u> from the sidelines.
10. After the race Kim drank an <u>amazingly</u> large amount of water.

EXERCISE B Underline each adverb and draw an arrow to the word it modifies.

11. Francis speaks Spanish <u>exceptionally</u> <u>well</u>.
12. Despite its bulk, a rhinoceros can move <u>amazingly</u> <u>quickly</u>.
13. The lion cubs approached the river <u>rather</u> <u>timidly</u>.
14. Joan drives the car <u>very</u> <u>skillfully</u>.
15. Are Artesian wells <u>much</u> deeper than other wells?
16. <u>Finally</u> the bus appeared in the distance.
17. I <u>recently</u> met my next-door neighbors.
18. Fog <u>frequently</u> drifts over San Francisco from the ocean.
19. The border between the United States and Canada is <u>unusually</u> long.
20. The ocean appears <u>somewhat</u> grayer on cloudy days.

CHAPTER 13 Adverbs and Adjectives

EXERCISE Underline the adjectives and adverbs in the following paragraph. Then write *adjective* (adj.) or *adverb* (adv.) above each one.

In her abstract paintings, the American artist Joan Mitchell uses bold, straight lines and a variety of organic and geometric shapes. Black, orange, blue, and white are the overwhelmingly predominant colors. These somewhat unusual color combinations may express her ambivalent feelings about nature. Her slashing and swooping brushstrokes express action and clearly convey power. Instead of being a simple and lyrical description of something, an expressionistic painting often reveals a painter's reaction to or a memory of something. Many artists choose a medium other than words to express their precise feelings. They believe that through their art, they can more clearly and effectively express their inner thoughts and changing emotions. The painter Mitchell was an artist whose passionate creations are highly prized in the finest art museums.

Name _____ Date _____

CHAPTER 13 Prepositions

[13E.1] A **preposition** shows the relationship between a noun or a pronoun and another word in the sentence.

> **EXERCISE** Choose the preposition or compound preposition in each sentence.

_____ 1. The meteor blazed across the sky.
  A The
  B blazed
  C across

_____ 2. We went home early on account of the weather.
  A early
  B on account of
  C the

_____ 3. Pine needles drop throughout the year.
  A needles
  B throughout
  C year

_____ 4. According to the last census, many people are moving south and west.
  A According to
  B to the last
  C moving

_____ 5. Sound travels very fast in water.
  A Sound
  B very
  C in

_____ 6. The football team won the game in the last few seconds.
  A The
  B in
  C few

_____ 7. The small hare was hiding underneath the leafy bush.
  A small
  B underneath
  C leafy

_____ 8. Despite the storm, the boys went out.
  A Despite
  B storm
  C out

_____ 9. You should not walk alone after dark.
  A not
  B alone
  C after

_____ 10. The tropical storm struck without a warning.
  A tropical
  B struck
  C without

_____ 11. The proud scientist marveled at his latest creation.
  A proud
  B marveled
  C at

_____ 12. The girl forgot about her math assignment last night.
  A about
  B math
  C last

_____ 13. After dinner the boys watched a science-fiction movie.
  A After
  B watched
  C a

_____ 14. The old, leather-bound books fell off the shelf.
  A leather-bound
  B fell
  C off

_____ 15. They left with the packages an hour ago.
  A with
  B an
  C ago

CHAPTER 13 Prepositions

EXERCISE Underline all the prepositions in each sentence.

1. Through the gate you will find three small children, and they will see the movie in the theater with you.

2. The girl named Sheryl went to the store around the corner.

3. He threw that new kind of baseball over the fence.

4. The foreman of the job ended his duties on December 3.

5. Please walk through the door, around the block, across the street, and out of the neighborhood!

6. From Room 121 came the sound of students cheering.

7. The dog inside the kennel is a rare breed of schnauzer.

8. The basketballs are under the stairs, and you should take them on your trip.

9. The three New Yorkers came bursting through the doors.

10. The students bought first-class seats for the trip to London.

11. During the night we watched the fireworks display from the roof.

12. You showed your scar, and the girl at the hospital looked away.

13. The flock of geese was last seen flying over Littletown.

14. By 7 p.m., many of the students had fallen asleep at their desks.

15. The couple across the street are the proud parents of a new baby boy.

16. Underneath the table you will find three different brands of shoes, but none of them are mine.

17. Her sprint around the track resulted in Mary's feeling sick to her stomach.

CHAPTER 13 Conjunctions

[13E.3] A **conjunction** connects words or groups of words.

EXERCISE Choose the coordinating conjunction or correlative conjunctions in each sentence.

_____ 1. Some people eat neither meat nor fish.
   A Some
   B neither/nor
   C fish

_____ 2. They can get protein from eggs or cheese.
   A can
   B from
   C or

_____ 3. Both cheese and beans contain protein.
   A Both/and
   B beans
   C contain

_____ 4. Soybeans are a valuable food, for they contain protein.
   A Soybeans
   B for
   C contain

_____ 5. No other vegetable, dried or fresh, contains so much protein.
   A No other
   B or
   C so

_____ 6. Soybeans come in various colors, but the yellow ones are most common.
   A in
   B but
   C most

_____ 7. They can be eaten as a vegetable or ground into flour.
   A as
   B or
   C into

_____ 8. They provide an inexpensive but nutritious diet for many people.
   A but
   B for
   C many

_____ 9. A healthy diet can prevent health problems such as anemia, cancer, and heart disease.
   A such as
   B anemia
   C and

_____ 10. Protein builds and repairs the body.
   A builds
   B and
   C the

_____ 11. Both fats and carbohydrates are also parts of a healthy diet.
   A Both/and
   B also
   C parts of

_____ 12. Either green or yellow vegetables are a good source of vitamin A.
   A Either/or
   B are
   C of

_____ 13. Fresh vegetables provide not only vitamins but also minerals.
   A not
   B but
   C not only/but also

_____ 14. Fruits, dried or fresh, are part of the human diet.
   A Fruits
   B or
   C part of

Name _____ Date _____

CHAPTER 13 Conjunctions and Interjections

[13E.5] An **interjection** is a word that expresses strong feeling or emotion.

> **EXERCISE** Underline and label all interjections (I) and conjunctions (C) in the following sentences.

1. Hooray! It has finally stopped raining.

2. Aha! I found my glasses on the floor, but they were broken.

3. Neither wild nor domestic animals eat such a variety of food as humans do.

4. Oh, there's a wasp!

5. I spilled the milk. Oops!

6. Carlos and Juan will ride their bikes to the park.

7. It is raining outside, yet the sun is shining.

8. I passed the test. Whew!

9. Whether to go to the pool or to the library is up to you.

10. All right! Did we really finish our project?

CHAPTER 13 Parts of Speech Review

EXERCISE Identify the part of speech for each of the underlined words: *noun, pronoun, adjective, adverb, verb, preposition, conjunction,* or *interjection*.

    Langston Hughes and Zora Neale Hurston are two of the most important writers to come out of the Harlem Renaissance, the **(1)** <u>artistic</u> movement that had its heyday in New York City in the first part of the 20th century. Hughes **(2)** <u>was raised</u> in the **(3)** <u>Midwest</u>, and Hurston was a product of a small, all-black town in Florida. Despite **(4)** <u>their</u> different backgrounds, both writers had parents who were **(5)** <u>fiercely</u> committed to their African American heritage. No doubt, this contributed to the writers' lifelong attention to capturing black life in their work. The Harlem of their day was a place where black artists and activists **(6)** <u>could thrive</u>, compose music, poetry, and plays. Hughes was celebrated for his jazz poetry, but he **(7)** <u>also</u> wrote novels, plays, essays, and short stories. Hurston, in addition to being a novelist, is known as a folklorist and a storyteller. *Their Eyes Were Watching God* is **(8)** <u>most</u> likely her best novel. Other leading writers in the Harlem literary movement included Richard Wright, Jean Toomer, **(9)** <u>and</u> Countee Cullen. Neither Toomer nor Cullen received the acclaim they deserved. Toomer's "Harvest Song" is a beautiful, evocative prose poem, **(10)** <u>one</u> deserving of the **(11)** <u>highest</u> praise. Literary scholars, culture historians, and people interested in the arts are amazed at the outpouring **(12)** <u>of</u> talent during the Harlem Renaissance. **(13)** <u>Alas</u>! Today, there **(14)** <u>is</u> no place similar to the Harlem of **(15)** <u>that</u> era, a "neighborhood" filled with geniuses.

1. _____
2. _____
3. _____
4. _____
5. _____
6. _____
7. _____
8. _____
9. _____
10. _____
11. _____
12. _____
13. _____
14. _____
15. _____

CHAPTER 14 Simple Subjects and Predicates

[14A.2] A **simple subject** is the main word in the complete subject.

EXERCISE A Choose the simple subject in each sentence.

_____ 1. California was at one time a British possession.
  A California
  B British

_____ 2. In 1936, Beryle Shinn picnicked on the shore north of San Francisco.
  A 1936
  B Beryle Shinn

_____ 3. He found a dirty old brass plate under a rock.
  A He
  B plate

_____ 4. Very meticulously, Beryle cleaned it with lots of soap and water.
  A Beryle
  B meticulously

_____ 5. A word was faintly visible.
  A A
  B word

EXERCISE B Underline the simple subject in each sentence.

6. The brass plate was apparently 357 years old.

7. Other scientists denounced the plate as a forgery.

8. Analysis of the metal showed its true age.

9. Plant cells on the metal were ancient.

10. The spelling of the words was typical of the spelling in Drake's day.

11. Finally the archaeologists accepted the plate as genuine.

12. That raised an interesting question.

13. Did California legally belong to Great Britain?

14. The discovery of the plate seemed to prove so.

Name _____ Date _____

CHAPTER 14 Simple Subjects and Predicates

[14A.2] A **simple predicate,** or **verb,** is the main word or phrase in the complete predicate.

EXERCISE A Choose the verb or verb phrase in each sentence.

_____ 1. Seventy percent of Earth's surface is covered by water.
  A is covered
  B by water

_____ 2. The floor of the ocean consists of mountains, canyons, and plains.
  A consists
  B plains

_____ 3. The tops of some mountains are islands.
  A tops
  B are

_____ 4. The Hawaiian volcano Mauna Kea rises 31,000 feet from the ocean floor.
  A rises
  B from

_____ 5. This surpasses Mount Everest by nearly 2,000 feet.
  A surpasses
  B nearly

_____ 6. In the Pacific the Mariana Trench lies seven miles deep.
  A lies
  B deep

EXERCISE B Underline the verb in each sentence. Circle the simple subject.

7. Recently scientists have discovered holes in the ocean floor.

8. Hot volcanic materials constantly flow out of these bodies.

9. Organisms convert the volcanic minerals into food.

10. Colonies of plants and animals flourish in these spots.

11. The Mediterranean was once a desert.

12. This desert lay 10,000 feet below the Atlantic Ocean.

13. Eons ago the ocean burst through.

14. The desert became the Mediterranean Sea.

Name _____ Date _____

CHAPTER 14 — Different Positions of Subjects

[14A.3] Inverted order means that the verb or part of a verb phrase comes before the subject.

> **EXERCISE A** Circle the subject in each sentence. The verb in each sentence is underlined. If the subject is understood, write (you) and circle it.

1. Under the sand on this beach <u>live</u> hundreds of ghost crabs.

2. Here by the Connecticut River <u>are</u> the footprints of dinosaurs.

3. <u>Read</u> a book each week during the summer.

4. There <u>are</u> a few dangerous spiders.

5. <u>Have</u> you ever <u>seen</u> a mole?

6. In midwinter on the top of Mount Washington <u>occur</u> truly arctic conditions.

7. Here in the Himalayas <u>live</u> the last wild snow leopards.

> **EXERCISE B** Underline the verb in each sentence. Then choose the subject of the sentence.

_____ 8. In the ocean near Seattle live giant octopuses.
  A ocean
  B octopuses

_____ 9. There must be many unknown plants in the Amazon Basin.
  A There
  B plants

_____ 10. Into the calm morning sky thundered the jet.
  A sky
  B jet

_____ 11. Have you ever been in a desert after a rain?
  A you
  B rain

_____ 12. A few feet above the English Channel flew the hovercraft.
  A English Channel
  B hovercraft

_____ 13. Have you heard of Mr. Bojangles?
  A you
  B Mr. Bojangles

_____ 14. Sign your name on the inside of this birthday card.
  A card
  B (You)

_____ 15. Did Texas ever belong to Mexico?
  A Texas
  B Mexico

24 Grade 11 • Chapter 14: The Sentence Base

Name _____ Date _____

CHAPTER 14 — Compound Subjects and Compound Verbs

[14A.5] A **compound subject** is two or more subjects in one sentence that have the same verb and are joined by a conjunction.

[14A.6] A **compound verb** is two or more verbs that have the same subject and are joined by a conjunction.

> **EXERCISE** Draw one line under each subject and two lines under each verb. Then decide whether the sentence has a compound subject, a compound verb, or both by writing the correct letter in the blank.

_____ 1. Neil and Sonya have picked blackberries and have made jam.
  A compound subject
  B compound verb
  C compound subject and compound verb

_____ 2. The Pacific Ocean and the Atlantic Ocean are joined by the Panama Canal but have different levels.
  A compound subject
  B compound verb
  C compound subject and compound verb

_____ 3. Queen Elizabeth I and Queen Victoria ruled for many years and were very popular sovereigns.
  A compound subject
  B compound verb
  C compound subject and compound verb

_____ 4. Driver ants and army ants conduct military campaigns.
  A compound subject
  B compound verb
  C compound subject and compound verb

_____ 5. The diver lowered herself into 100 feet of water and spotted an eel.
  A compound subject
  B compound verb
  C compound subject and compound verb

_____ 6. Apples are grown all around the world and have been found in prehistoric dwellings.
  A compound subject
  B compound verb
  C compound subject and compound verb

_____ 7. The jet glided to the ground and came to a stop.
  A compound subject
  B compound verb
  C compound subject and compound verb

_____ 8. Oak and locust are two slow-burning woods.
  A compound subject
  B compound verb
  C compound subject and compound verb

CHAPTER 14 Sentence Fragments

[14B] A **sentence fragment** is a group of words that does not express a complete thought.

EXERCISE A Label each group of words S for sentence or F for fragment.

_____ 1. You will read *Tender Is the Night*, a novel by F. Scott Fitzgerald.

_____ 2. A strange incident of theft in 1986, when a lock of George Washington's hair was stolen from a French museum.

_____ 3. More sheep than humans in the country of Australia.

_____ 4. Unfortunately, this cottage cheese will have to be thrown away.

_____ 5. Max, Molly, and Buddy, the three most common names for dogs.

_____ 6. To date, no one has been nominated for an Academy Award more times than Meryl Streep.

_____ 7. According to my aunt, the rutabaga, a tasty vegetable.

_____ 8. Have you listened to the music of Charles Mingus?

_____ 9. This nectarine, for example, will give you quick energy before the game.

_____ 10. A bracelet made of a material called bakelite.

EXERCISE B The following passage contains four sentence fragments. Underline each fragment. On the lines below, rewrite each fragment so that it is a complete sentence.

Imagine the courage of those. Who first experimented with parachutes! Early experiments, such as the one by L.S. Lenormand in 1783, showed exceptional daring. Lenormand was the first to demonstrate a parachute in action. Fourteen years later, A.J. Garnerin jumped 3,000 feet. By 1802, had increased the height of his jumps to 8,000 feet. Early parachutes were constructed of canvas. Which was later to become silk and ultimately nylon. Today, parachutes made out of "super-synthetics" help land space capsules on the moon.

_____
_____
_____
_____
_____
_____

Name _____ Date _____

CHAPTER 14 — Direct Objects

[14C.1] A **direct object** is a noun or a pronoun that receives the action of the verb.

> **EXERCISE A** Choose the direct object in each sentence. A sentence may have more than one direct object.

_____ 1. Eli Whitney invented the cotton gin in 1793.
    A Eli Whitney
    B cotton gin
    C 1793

_____ 2. Tokyo and Stockholm have audible traffic signals.
    A Stockholm
    B traffic
    C signals

_____ 3. Peggy, did you see that huge hailstone?
    A you
    B that
    C hailstone

_____ 4. People make cocoa from the seeds of the cacao tree.
    A cocoa
    B seeds
    C tree

_____ 5. We used rollers and paintbrushes on the living room walls.
    A rollers
    B paintbrushes
    C rollers, paintbrushes

_____ 6. The coelacanth fish has a brain that is remarkably smaller than its body.
    A brain
    B smaller
    C body

> **EXERCISE B** Underline the direct object in each of the following sentences. Some sentences contain more than one direct object.

7. Pauline caught a nineteen-inch pickerel on her first cast.
8. Peter picked carrots and lettuce.
9. The mourning dove has a sad call.
10. How many hours per week do you watch television?
11. James Michener has written books about several countries.
12. Ts'ai Lun invented paper in China about A.D. 105.
13. The bloodhound led the detectives to the secret hideout.
14. A typical plant receives only partial nutrition from the soil.
15. I would like to write a novel or a play.

Name _____ Date _____

CHAPTER 14 Indirect Objects

[14C.2] An **indirect object** answers the question *To* or *for whom?* or *To* or *for what?* after an action verb.

EXERCISE A Choose the indirect object in each sentence. If there is no indirect object, choose *no indirect object*.

_____ 1. The winner of the race showed the spectators her medal.
  A spectators
  B medal

_____ 2. The manager sold us the videocassette recorder for half price.
  A us
  B recorder

_____ 3. After the rock concert, Joel gave his tape to me.
  A me
  B no indirect object

_____ 4. Please don't send me any mail by special delivery.
  A me
  B mail

_____ 5. Uncle Harold gave Marjorie money for a ten-speed bike.
  A money
  B Marjorie

_____ 6. Offer that man twenty dollars for his old lawn mower.
  A man
  B dollars

EXERCISE B In each sentence, underline each indirect object and write IO above it. Some sentences may have more than one.

7. The sudden draft gave Len a chill.

8. Sue gave her mother a birthday card.

9. Mrs. Mason gave her son some cheese made of reindeer milk.

10. Roman emperors paid their soldiers salt for their services.

11. Show us the site of your new home.

12. Camel caravans brought Africans goods from the Sahara.

13. The instructor taught his students the first step in using the equipment.

14. Please buy me a new battery for my calculator.

15. The store charged my family and me too much for the merchandise.

CHAPTER 14 Direct and Indirect Objects

EXERCISE A Underline each direct and indirect object. Then label each one DO (direct object) or IO (indirect object).

1. Paul gave Carol a ticket to the concert.

2. Don't tell anyone my secret.

3. He e-mailed me a picture of the two of us at the concert.

4. The pop fly hit my mother and two other spectators at the ballgame.

5. My sister gave a speech at the last political convention.

6. The speaker handed me the microphone.

7. They invited us to their victory celebration.

8. The usher found me a seat up in the nosebleed section of the bleachers.

9. I painted my deck with a sealant to prevent rain from rotting the wood.

10. Please show Dad your entry for the art contest.

EXERCISE B Using the verbs below, write sentences with at least one indirect object and one direct object. Write IO above each indirect object and DO above each direct object.

Example: offer I offered John a peach.   (IO: John, DO: peach)

sent _____

teach _____

show _____

CHAPTER 14 Objective Complements

[14C.3] An **objective complement** is a noun or an adjective that renames or describes the direct object.

EXERCISE A Underline the direct object in each sentence. Then choose the objective complement. If a sentence contains no objective complement, choose *no objective complement*.

_____ 1. Hank considered gliders dangerous.
   A gliders
   B dangerous
   C no objective complement

_____ 2. The members unanimously named her leader of the club.
   A her
   B leader
   C no objective complement

_____ 3. Sasha considers horses intelligent.
   A intelligent
   B horses
   C no objective complement

_____ 4. Grace painted her bookcase mauve.
   A bookcase
   B mauve
   C no objective complement

_____ 5. The electoral college elected George Bush president.
   A president
   B George Bush
   C no objective complement

_____ 6. The club members considered her competent.
   A her
   B competent
   C no objective complement

EXERCISE B Underline the objective complement in each sentence. Then draw an arrow to the direct object it renames or describes.

7. The solarium keeps our living room warm.

8. The trainer unleashed all the dogs, large and small.

9. The legislature elected a former nun House Speaker.

10. The musicians named Stuart conductor of their band.

CHAPTER 14 Subject Complements

[14C.4] Subject complements complete the meaning of linking verbs. There are two kinds of subject complements—predicate nominatives and predicate adjectives.

EXERCISE A Write PN if the underlined word in each sentence is a predicate nominative or PA if the underlined word is a predicate adjective.

_____ 1. Ronald Reagan was once a movie <u>actor</u>.

_____ 2. The first one out of the room was <u>Beth</u>.

_____ 3. The freshly cut grass smelled <u>sweet</u>.

_____ 4. A most infamous character in the play *Othello* is <u>Iago</u>.

_____ 5. Contrary to some reports, Albert Einstein was <u>brilliant</u>.

_____ 6. The name Don Quixote is <u>famous</u> in many countries.

_____ 7. James Monroe was the fourth <u>president</u> from Virginia.

_____ 8. That is <u>Rachel</u> with the ball.

_____ 9. Yorkshire pudding is a <u>kind</u> of large popover.

_____ 10. She felt <u>fine</u> this morning.

EXERCISE B Underline the subject complement in each sentence. Label it as a predicate nominative (PN) or a predicate adjective (PA).

_____ 11. Mary McLeon Bethune was ambitious.

_____ 12. Mrs. Merryweather was our substitute math teacher for a month.

_____ 13. Although many people fear snakes, most snakes are harmless.

_____ 14. The official flower of November is the chrysanthemum.

_____ 15. Dozens of kinds of cereal are available in the supermarket.

_____ 16. Derek Jacobi is a brilliant performer.

_____ 17. Randolph's daydreams are habitual.

_____ 18. The elephant's ears are fanlike.

_____ 19. The cloth feels rather fuzzy.

_____ 20. That is one strong woman.

CHAPTER 14 Sentence Patterns

EXERCISE A For the following sentences underline all complements and label as direct object (DO), indirect object (IO), objective complement (OC), predicate adjective (PA), or predicate nominative (PN).

_____ 1. The worst plant is poison ivy.

_____ 2. The mint in our garden smells spicy.

_____ 3. Text me your answer to my question.

_____ 4. The United States elected Barack Obama president in 2008.

_____ 5. The dodo and the passenger pigeon became extinct years ago.

_____ 6. Abraham Lincoln's character can be an inspiration for all of us.

_____ 7. I wrote the company a letter to complain about their poor customer service.

_____ 8. Big, dark sunglasses are now a popular accessory.

_____ 9. She felt sick after eating twelve hot dogs in one sitting.

_____ 10. Extreme cold can turn your lips blue.

EXERCISE B Write the appropriate sentence pattern in the blank. Choose from S-V; S-V-O; S-V-I-O; S-V-O-C; S-V-A; or S-V-N.

_____ 11. The sunrise on the ranch is a beautiful sight.

_____ 12. Never give your older sister advice on how to dress.

_____ 13. Yesterday Manuel took the dogs on a long walk.

_____ 14. Some fans in the crowd painted their faces purple.

_____ 15. She went to the library to gather information for her project.

_____ 16. Johnny Depp was perfect as the zany character of Willy Wonka in the movie _Charlie and the Chocolate Factory_.

Name _____ Date _____

CHAPTER 14 Sentence Base Review

EXERCISE Read the passage and answer the questions that follow.

(1) Each year, two million tourists visit Mount Rushmore National Park in the Black Hills of South Dakota. (2) The park contains a unique historical <u>monument</u>. (3) This monument consists of huge sculptures of the heads of four important U.S. presidents. (4) Amazingly, each head is sixty feet high. (5) Carved out of the granite mountain. (6) These four presidents made tremendous contributions to their country. (7) Washington was a Revolutionary War general and served as our first official head of state. (8) Jefferson is most <u>famous</u> for having written the Declaration of Independence. (9) Lincoln is revered for his part in keeping the United States from splitting into two separate nations at the time of the Civil War. (10) Theodore Roosevelt is a <u>hero</u> to many because he led the "impossible" task of building the Panama Canal. (11) However, controversy will always swirl around this national memorial. (12) The reason being that for the Lakota Sioux Indian tribe, the Black Hills setting is <u>sacred</u>. (13) White explorers renamed this mountain "<u>Rushmore</u>." (14) However, it was known first to the Sioux as "Six Grandfathers."

1. What is the simple subject in sentence 1? _____

2. In sentence 2, the underlined word is a _____.
      A direct object   **B** objective complement   **C** predicate nominative   **D** predicate adjective

3. What is the complete predicate in sentence 3?_____
   _____

4. What is the best way to combine sentences 4 and 5? _____
      A Amazingly, each head is sixty feet high, carved out of the granite mountain.
      B Amazingly, each head is sixty feet high and is carved out of the granite mountain.
      C Amazingly, each head is sixty feet high but is carved out of the granite mountain.
      D Amazingly, each head is sixty feet high; carved out of the granite mountain.

5. What is the direct object in sentence 6? _____

6. Sentence 7 has a _____.
      A simple subject   **B** compound subject   **C** compound verb   **D** compound subject and compound verb

7. The underlined word in sentence 8 is a _____.
      A direct object   **B** indirect object   **C** predicate nominative   **D** predicate adjective

continued

Chapter 14: Sentence Base Review *continued*

8. What is the simple predicate in sentence 9? _____

9. In sentence 10, the underlined word is a _____.
   A direct object   **B** indirect object   **C** predicate nominative   **D** predicate adjective

10. What is the simple subject in sentence 11? _____

11. In sentence 12, the underlined word is a _____.
    A direct object   **B** indirect object   **C** predicate nominative   **D** predicate adjective

12. In sentence 13, the underlined word is a _____.
    A direct object   **B** objective complement   **C** predicate nominative   **D** predicate adjective

Name _____ Date _____

CHAPTER 15 Prepositional Phrases

[15A] A **phrase** is a group of related words that function as a single part of speech. A phrase does not have a subject and a verb. A **prepositional phrase** begins with a preposition and ends with a noun or a pronoun, called the **object of the preposition**.

EXERCISE A Choose the word or words the underlined prepositional phrase modifies in each sentence.

_____ 1. Arthur was a legendary king <u>of the British people</u>.
   A Arthur
   B king

_____ 2. Britain had no king <u>at that time</u>.
   A had
   B king

_____ 3. One day a huge stone appeared <u>outside a church</u>.
   A stone
   B appeared

_____ 4. A sword was stuck <u>in the stone</u>.
   A was stuck
   B sword

_____ 5. Only Arthur could pull it out <u>of the stone</u>.
   A could pull
   B out

_____ 6. Thus he was crowned king <u>of Britain</u>.
   A was crowned
   B king

EXERCISE B Underline the prepositional phrase in each sentence. Then draw an arrow to the word or words it modifies.

7. Arthur and his knights fought evil and rescued people in distress.

8. The sorcerer Merlin helped King Arthur in the defeat of his enemies.

9. Arthur's half sister Morgana was also an enemy of his.

10. King Arthur was wounded in a fight.

11. A mysterious lady carried the wounded king to safety.

12. At his death the Lady of the Lake brought King Arthur to a land called Avalon.

13. Many books tell of King Arthur's adventures.

Name _____   Date _____

CHAPTER 15 Prepositional Phrases

[15A.1] An **adjectival phrase** is a prepositional phrase that is used to modify a noun or a pronoun.
[15A.2] An **adverbial phrase** is a prepositional phrase that is used to modify a verb, an adjective, or an adverb.

EXERCISE A If the underlined prepositional phrase is an adjectival phrase, write ADJ in the blank. If it is an adverbial phrase, write ADV.

_____ 1. Antelopes are animals <u>like deer</u>.

_____ 2. They have an even number <u>of hoofed toes</u>.

_____ 3. They grow only one pair <u>of horns</u>.

_____ 4. Africa is the home <u>of many antelopes</u>.

_____ 5. Great herds graze <u>on the plains</u>.

_____ 6. The antelopes will run <u>for their lives</u>.

EXERCISE B Underline the prepositional phrase in each sentence. Draw an arrow to the word or words it modifies. Finally, label it ADJ for adjectival or ADV for adverbial.

_____ 7. The sable antelope has four-foot-long horns on its head.

_____ 8. The sable lives in southern and eastern Africa.

_____ 9. Gazelles live in both Africa and Asia.

_____ 10. They are medium-sized animals with lyre-shaped horns.

_____ 11. The springbok gazelle can spring ten feet into the air.

_____ 12. The tiny duiker could sit in your lap.

_____ 13. Among the largest antelopes are the wildebeests and hartebeests.

_____ 14. The pronghorn antelope of North America is not a true antelope.

_____ 15. It is also known as the prairie ghost.

_____ 16. The bucks use their horns in the challenge of their rivals.

Name _____ Date _____

CHAPTER 15 Appositives and Appositive Phrases

[15B] An **appositive** is a noun or a pronoun that identifies or explains another noun or pronoun in the sentence.

[15B.1] An appositive and its modifiers are called an **appositive phrase**.

> **EXERCISE** Choose the word or words the underlined appositive or appositive phrase modifies in each sentence.

_____ 1. Life on Earth, <u>the watery planet</u>, depends on water.
   A Life
   B Earth

_____ 2. Water is created by a chemical reaction between two gases, <u>hydrogen and oxygen</u>.
   A reaction
   B gases

_____ 3. The oceans, <u>97.2 percent of Earth's water</u>, are salty.
   A oceans
   B salty

_____ 4. Liquid water, <u>a substance required by all living things</u>, allows life on Earth to exist.
   A Liquid
   B water

_____ 5. The blue whale, <u>the largest known animal to live on sea or land</u>, weighs several tons.
   A several tons
   B blue whale

_____ 6. Giant tubeworms and mussels live near hydrothermal vents, <u>cracks in the ocean floor</u>.
   A mussels
   B vents

_____ 7. Europa, <u>one of Jupiter's moons</u>, may have an ocean of liquid water beneath its icy crust.
   A Europa
   B crust

_____ 8. The Mid-Ocean Ridge, <u>Earth's longest mountain range</u>, is under the ocean.
   A Mid-Ocean Ridge
   B ocean

_____ 9. El Niño, <u>a cyclic shift of warm waters across the Pacific Ocean</u>, has dramatic effects on the world's climate.
   A El Niño
   B climate

_____ 10. Venezuela's Angel Falls, <u>the tallest waterfall in the world</u>, measures more than half a mile.
   A Venezuela's
   B Angel Falls

CHAPTER 15 Appositives and Appositive Phrases

EXERCISE Underline the appositives or appositive phrases in the following paragraph. Draw an arrow to the word or words they modify.

Ice caps, <u>2.15 percent of the total amount of Earth's water</u>, hold water in a solid state. Two million cubic miles of water, <u>Earth's reserve supply</u>, is underground. In the upper layer, <u>the aeration zone</u>, water is absorbed by plants. In the lower layer, <u>the saturation zone</u>, the water feeds lakes, swamps, rivers, and wells. The Sahara, <u>a desert with almost no visible water</u>, has an enormous underground reservoir. The atmosphere, <u>the area above Earth's surface</u>, holds only 3,100 cubic miles of water. Clouds, <u>condensed water vapor</u>, inhabit the upper atmosphere. Fog, <u>also condensed water vapor</u>, is really just low-lying clouds. Acid rain, <u>a consequence of sulfur and nitrogen air pollutants</u>, threatens Earth's environment. What should be a vital part of the Earth's system of replenishment, rainfall, has become deadly.

Name _____ Date _____

CHAPTER 15 Punctuation with Appositives and Appositive Phrases

If an appositive contains information essential to the meaning of a sentence, no punctuation is needed.

If an appositive or appositive phrase contains nonessential information, a comma or commas should be used to separate it from the rest of the sentence.

EXERCISE Underline the appositive or appositive phrase in each sentence. Then label it as essential (E) or nonessential (N). Finally, add commas to set off the nonessential clauses.

_____ 1. Steve Prefontaine an exceptional runner won fourteen U.S. track and field records before his death at the age of twenty-four.

_____ 2. He was born in Coos Bay a small town in Oregon.

_____ 3. In high school he was coached by Walter McClure a former track star.

_____ 4. At the age of twenty-one he competed at one Olympiad the 1972 Summer Games in Munich.

_____ 5. Many people also enjoy long-distance running a popular method for improving cardiovascular fitness.

_____ 6. The movie *Chariots of Fire* is about two British sprinters competing in the 1924 Olympics.

_____ 7. New runners especially those who are overweight should not strain themselves.

_____ 8. Bess Truman the star athlete of her class in finishing school was the wife of this country's thirty-third president.

_____ 9. Sarah Knox Polk the First Lady from 1845 to 1849 opened the Executive Mansion to the public.

_____ 10. First Lady Michelle Obama graduated from Princeton University and Harvard Law School.

CHAPTER 15 Punctuation with Appositives and Appositive Phrases

EXERCISE Each sentence contains an appositive phrase. Underline the appositive and then add or cross out commas where needed.

1. Edward P. Weston, a long-distance walker, lived in New England in 1860.

2. Weston's first walk, a 478-mile journey, was from Boston to Washington.

3. This trip, the result of an election bet, took ten days.

4. Presidential candidate Abraham Lincoln had just won the election.

5. A number of spectators, well-wishers in horse-drawn buggies, accompanied Weston.

6. In one village the townspeople gave him handshakes, presents for the new president.

7. A delay, a serious one, occurred because of foot-deep snow.

8. Weston's periods of sleep, often catnaps in farmhouse kitchens, were few and brief.

9. His longest rest, a snooze of six hours, was in a New Jersey inn.

10. His meals, sandwiches and pastries, were eaten on the road.

11. The new president Lincoln had already been sworn in.

12. For this first walk Weston received a prize, a bag of peanuts.

13. Weston, a clever man, never again walked for peanuts.

14. His next long walk, a hike from Maine to Chicago, took twenty-six days.

15. News of this hike, a feature in most newspapers, made him famous.

Name _____ Date _____

CHAPTER 15 Participles and Participial Phrases

[15C.1] A **participle** is a verb form that is used as an adjective.
[15C.3] A **participial phrase** is a participle with its modifiers and complements—all working together as an adjective.

> **EXERCISE A** Choose the word the underlined participial phrase modifies in each sentence.

_____ 1. The snails <u>seen in our garden</u> have relatives everywhere.
    A snails
    B relatives

_____ 2. <u>Built for endurance, not speed</u>, snails are hardy.
    A snails
    B hardy

_____ 3. <u>Retreating into its shell</u>, the snail has a safe refuge.
    A snail
    B refuge

_____ 4. A snail <u>displayed in the British Museum</u> emerged from its shell four years later.
    A snail
    B shell

_____ 5. <u>Found all over the globe</u>, snails are very prolific.
    A snails
    B prolific

_____ 6. One tiny variety <u>located originally in Florida</u> is now found all over South America.
    A tiny
    B variety

_____ 7. In the spring you can hear the Burgundy snail <u>humming a tune</u>.
    A spring
    B snail

> **EXERCISE B** Underline the participial phrase in each sentence and draw an arrow to the word it modifies.

8. This animal, pulling a shell nearly 400 times its own weight, is like a baby dragging a chair.

9. A snail, using a retractable radula, scrapes food into its mouth.

10. Rising early, I saw the sun come up.

11. Having a good sense of direction, Ilona rarely gets lost.

12. Shopping in a mall, you can buy anything.

13. Having the advantage of electric lights, Americans today stay up later than their ancestors did.

14. Inventing the decimal system about A.D. 800, the Hindus presented civilization with a great gift.

CHAPTER 15 — Participles and Participial Phrases

EXERCISE For each sentence, underline the participial phrase. Draw an arrow to the word it modifies.

1. Using cesium atoms, a clock gains one second in 300 years.

2. The cars passing by are filled with commuters.

3. Having unlisted telephone numbers, 25 million U.S. citizens preserve their privacy.

4. Sailing in his hang glider, Joel saw the countryside beneath him.

5. Mowing the lawn in my shorts, I was bitten by mosquitoes.

6. Family names derived from people's surroundings were common in the Middle Ages.

7. Someone living near a hill or mountain might be called Hill in England or DuMont in France.

8. People named Wood, Stone, Lake, Brook, or Forest probably come from families that lived near those natural features.

9. Being unable to read, most people in the Middle Ages often relied on pictures.

10. A sign picturing an animal or object would identify an inn or a shop.

11. A shop identified by a bell or a star could give a name to its owner.

12. Working or living there, a person might become known as Mr. or Miss Bell or Mr. or Mrs. Star.

13. Names based on people's hometowns were common too.

14. Most English names ending in *-ton*, *-ham*, or *-wich* come from the names of towns.

15. The mother caught her merry children jumping on the bed.

CHAPTER 15 Punctuation with Participial Phrases

EXERCISE A Write E if the underlined phrase is essential and N if it is nonessential. Then add commas as needed.

_____ 1. The runner coming in my direction eyed me sharply.

_____ 2. The box dropped from the helicopter contained food.

_____ 3. That cat lying in the sunlight is not ours.

_____ 4. Those clouds piling up over the peaks look ominous.

_____ 5. The chameleon turning from tan to green became invisible.

_____ 6. Juan saw many young trees growing on the hillside.

_____ 7. Tiny insects flitting before his eyes annoyed the hiker.

EXERCISE B Underline the participial phrases. Use commas to set off nonessential phrases. If no commas are needed, write *none* after the sentence.

8. Our plane flying into the storm was peppered by hailstones.

9. Flying higher the heron circled over the swamp.

10. Mangrove swamps once considered wastelands, are full of life.

11. Reaching down into the mud mangrove tree roots are like fingers.

12. Being able to live in saltwater these trees flourish along the Florida coast.

13. Snakes and tree crabs living in the branches populate vast areas.

14. Almost 200 species of birds including many rare ones, roost there.

15. Loons and grebes migrating from the North winter here.

16. The branches forming a dense canopy, serve as flight platforms for pelicans and herons.

17. Hiding underneath the bush the big cat was not visible to its predators.

Name _____ Date _____

CHAPTER 15 — Gerunds and Gerund Phrases

[15C.4] A **gerund** is a verb form that is used as a noun.
[15C.5] A **gerund phrase** is a gerund with its modifiers and complements all working together as a noun.

EXERCISE A Identify the underlined part of each sentence as a *verb* (V) or a *gerund* (G).

_____ 1. Running fast makes your heart beat rapidly.

_____ 2. He gives cooking on a barbecue his devoted attention.

_____ 3. Rudy enjoys preparing gourmet meals for guests.

_____ 4. She is exercising so vigorously because she wants to get her heart rate up.

_____ 5. Sitting in a whirlpool bath is a relaxing experience.

_____ 6. I enjoy my hobby, and I am planning on doing it for many more years.

_____ 7. A popular exercise fad from the 1980s was hanging upside down by one's ankles.

_____ 8. Doesn't everybody enjoy going on a vacation?

_____ 9. Walking downhill is hard on aging knees.

_____ 10. Oh, no, my dog is getting into the garbage can.

EXERCISE B Underline the gerund phrase in each of the following sentences.

11. My least favorite chore is putting away dishes every evening.

12. Running a mile a day is an ongoing effort.

13. Making coffee may not be as easy as you think.

14. Painting a room can be a dreadful chore.

15. Waiting patiently in the outer office was never easy for Yoko.

16. Wearing an old pair of socks over your shoes will keep your shoes clean.

17. The crying girl could not remember giving away her book.

18. Have you tried taping the pictures onto the painted cardboard?

19. Tongs should make the process of barbecuing chicken easier.

20. Some nutritionists are advocating eating an all-protein diet.

CHAPTER 15   Gerunds and Gerund Phrases

EXERCISE A Identify each underlined gerund phrase as a subject, direct object, indirect object, object of a preposition, predicate nominative, or appositive.

_____ 1. The practice of <u>naming people for their occupations</u> was also common during medieval times.
   A object of a preposition
   B predicate nominative
   C appositive

_____ 2. <u>Explaining the origin of Miller, Carpenter, or Taylor</u> is not difficult.
   A subject
   B direct object
   C indirect object

_____ 3. <u>Shortening Blacksmith to Smith</u> was a frequent practice.
   A subject
   B direct object
   C indirect object

_____ 4. Just as common was <u>naming people for their ancestors</u>.
   A subject
   B predicate nominative
   C appositive

_____ 5. <u>Identifying people by a physical characteristic</u> was often necessary.
   A subject
   B direct object
   C indirect object

EXERCISE B Underline the gerund phrase. Then identify each underlined gerund phrase as a subject, direct object, object of a preposition, predicate nominative, or appositive.

_____ 8. People started using adjectives like *short* and *large* together with first names.

_____ 9. Applying this practice to redheaded people resulted in names like Reid and Reed.

_____ 10. Many Americans today visit the countries of their ancestors for one purpose, tracing their origins.

_____ 11. My favorite way to spend a Saturday is volunteering at the animal shelter.

_____ 12. Mount Vesuvius destroyed Pompeii by burying it under ashes and mud.

_____ 13. Many architects advocate designing solar-heated homes.

_____ 14. Jules Verne exercised a unique ability, envisioning scientific inventions of the future.

Name _____   Date _____

CHAPTER 15 — Infinitives and Infinitive Phrases

[15C.6] An **infinitive** is a verb form that usually begins with *to* and is used as a noun, an adjective, or an adverb.

[15C.7] An **infinitive phrase** is an infinitive with its modifiers and complements all working together as a noun, an adjective, or an adverb.

EXERCISE A Identify whether the underlined infinitive phrase in each sentence is used as a noun, an adjective, or an adverb.

_____ 1. Scientists hope <u>to find a cure for the common cold</u>.

_____ 2. The best place <u>to see the Olympic Range</u> is on the Hurricane Ridge Road.

_____ 3. Charles Lindbergh was the first person <u>to fly alone across the Atlantic</u>.

_____ 4. Wasps are starting <u>to build a nest in our garage</u>.

_____ 5. The coach asked me <u>to run a mile</u>.

_____ 6. Conservationists hope <u>to save the California condor from extinction</u>.

_____ 7. TV cameras have zoom lenses <u>to bring the action closer</u>.

_____ 8. The flute was one of the first instruments <u>to be used in Western music</u>.

EXERCISE B Underline the infinitive or infinitive phrase in each of the following sentences. Then determine whether it is used as a noun, an adjective, or an adverb.

_____ 9. Fran tried to help Mike with his science project.

_____ 10. Scuba divers are hired to search for ancient Greek and Roman shipwrecks.

_____ 11. It takes hard work to wax a car properly.

_____ 12. Gilbert Stuart was happy to entertain his friends lavishly.

_____ 13. Van Meegeren attempted to forge many well-known paintings.

_____ 14. The dike was built to keep seawater out of the fields.

_____ 15. Jerry offered one way to settle the argument.

CHAPTER 15 — Participles, Gerunds, and Infinitives

EXERCISE For each of the following sentences, decide if the underlined part is a prepositional, participial, gerund, or infinitive phrase.

_____ 1. You are free <u>to do as you choose</u>.
    A prepositional   **B** participial   **C** gerund   **D** infinitive

_____ 2. <u>Objecting to the eagle on the national emblem</u>, Benjamin Franklin suggested the wild turkey instead.
    A prepositional   **B** participial   **C** gerund   **D** infinitive

_____ 3. <u>Running inventories</u> is a typical way that a mainframe computer is used in large corporations.
    A prepositional   **B** participial   **C** gerund   **D** infinitive

_____ 4. When the time comes <u>to produce a final copy</u>, the printer performs the task automatically.
    A prepositional   **B** participial   **C** gerund   **D** infinitive

_____ 5. A mouse, <u>rolled over a flat surface</u>, may be used to move a cursor on the monitor.
    A prepositional   **B** participial   **C** gerund   **D** infinitive

_____ 6. There is no need <u>to make your own butter</u>.
    A prepositional   **B** participial   **C** gerund   **D** infinitive

_____ 7. <u>Viewed from a distance</u>, the American eagle looks bald.
    A prepositional   **B** participial   **C** gerund   **D** infinitive

_____ 8. Besides keyboards, many other techniques exist for <u>inputting data</u>.
    A prepositional   **B** participial   **C** gerund   **D** infinitive

_____ 9. If we found a training class, he might be persuaded <u>to join us</u>.
    A prepositional   **B** participial   **C** gerund   **D** infinitive

_____ 10. We walked <u>to the store</u> instead of driving our car.
    A prepositional   **B** participial   **C** gerund   **D** infinitive

_____ 11. <u>Riding your bike to work</u> is a great way to get exercise and help the environment.
    A prepositional   **B** participial   **C** gerund   **D** infinitive

_____ 12. My dog, <u>startled by the loud fireworks</u>, ran into the street.
    A prepositional   **B** participial   **C** gerund   **D** infinitive

_____ 13. <u>On the other side</u> of the school is a large open courtyard.
    A prepositional   **B** participial   **C** gerund   **D** infinitive

_____ 14. <u>Talking on her cell phone while driving</u>, Gabriella ran into a telephone pole.
    A prepositional   **B** participial   **C** gerund   **D** infinitive

_____ 15. Carrie lost five pounds by <u>eating fresh vegetables instead of junk food</u>.
    A prepositional   **B** participial   **C** gerund   **D** infinitive

Name _____ Date _____

CHAPTER 15 — Misplaced and Dangling Modifiers

[15D.1] A modifier that is placed too far away from the word it modifies is called a **misplaced modifier**.
[15D.2] A **dangling modifier** is a phrase that is used as a modifier but does not describe any word in the sentence.

EXERCISE A If the following sentences contain a misplaced or dangling modifier, write I (incorrect). Write C (correct) if the sentence is correct.

_____ 1. We missed the opening piece arriving late to the concert.

_____ 2. Looking in the showroom window, the latest car models hypnotized Eric.

_____ 3. To germinate properly, tomato seeds need warm days and cool nights.

_____ 4. I could see two squirrels gathering acorns gazing through my window.

_____ 5. Scurrying beneath the sand, we saw dozens of mole crabs.

_____ 6. Baked to a crispy brown, Beth took the pies out of the oven.

_____ 7. We saw three fires flying over the forest.

_____ 8. The French established a trade with the Indians in furs.

EXERCISE B Rewrite the incorrect sentences above so that they are correct.

_____
_____
_____
_____
_____
_____
_____
_____
_____
_____
_____
_____

Name _____   Date _____

CHAPTER 15 Phrases Review

EXERCISE A Identify each of the following underlined phrases as a prepositional (PREP), appositive (A), participial (PART), gerund (G), or infinitive (I) phrase.

A properly cut diamond is valued **(1)** by people all over the world. Many of the world's diamonds are from Cape Colony **(2)** a province in South Africa. In 1866 a young South African boy **(3)** Eramus Jacob was watching his father's sheep. **(4)** Seeing a transparent stone on the bank of the Orange River Jacob picked it up. This pretty pebble turned out **(5)** to be a 21-carat diamond.

Local farmers began **(6)** panning for diamonds along the banks of the Orange River. Then in 1869, another shepherd boy found an 83-carat diamond **(7)** the famous Star of South Africa. With this discovery, **(8)** hunting for diamonds became more than just a hobby.

Early prospectors found many diamonds in a layer of clay close to the surface. By **(9)** digging a few feet into the ground, prospectors found a greater quantity of higher-quality diamonds. In 1871, some men **(10)** digging a well for water discovered an 87-carat diamond seventy-six feet below the surface. Thus, diamond seeking became diamond mining, with mining companies **(11)** probing deep into the earth. Today 1,000 tons of soil must be moved **(12)** to find an ounce of diamonds.

1. _____
2. _____
3. _____
4. _____
5. _____
6. _____

7. _____
8. _____
9. _____
10. _____
11. _____
12. _____

EXERCISE B Some of the phrases in the paragraph above need commas. On the lines below, rewrite any sentences so that the phrases are correctly punctuated. If the phrase is correctly punctuated as is, write C on the line.

13. Phrase 1 _____

14. Phrase 2 _____

15. Phrase 3 _____

16. Phrase 4 _____

17. Phrase 5 _____

continued

Name _____ Date _____

Chapter 15: Phrases Review *continued*

18. Phrase 6 _____

19. Phrase 7 _____

20. Phrase 8 _____

21. Phrase 9 _____

22. Phrase 10 _____

23. Phrase 11 _____

24. Phrase 12 _____

Name _____   Date _____

CHAPTER 16 — Independent and Subordinate Clauses

[16A] A **clause** is a group of words that has a subject and a verb.

[16A.1] An **independent (main)** clause can stand alone as a sentence because it expresses a complete thought.

[16A.2] A **subordinate (dependent)** clause cannot stand alone because it does not express a complete thought.

EXERCISE A Write **I** if the underlined clause is independent and **S** if it is subordinate.

_____ 1. Sections of bamboo make a pleasing clacking sound <u>when they are hung as wind chimes</u>.

_____ 2. <u>Botanists have named about 200 species of bamboo</u>, some of which grow 100 feet high.

_____ 3. One variety is so hard <u>that it makes sparks when struck</u>.

_____ 4. Many people use bamboo screens <u>that roll up and down</u>.

_____ 5. Some people use bamboo fishing rods, and <u>others carry bamboo canes</u>.

_____ 6. Bamboo is the fastest growing plant <u>that we know</u>.

_____ 7. There are varieties <u>that grow four feet every twenty-four hours</u>.

_____ 8. Bamboo spreads quickly, <u>since new plants shoot up from the roots of older plants</u>.

_____ 9. <u>The young shoots of some varieties are cut</u> when they first appear.

_____ 10. <u>After the outer layer is peeled off</u>, they are fried or boiled.

EXERCISE B Underline the independent clauses in the following paragraph.

The Japanese have more uses for bamboo than any other people do. They fashion it into chopsticks, and they also make flutes out of it. Bamboo was imported from Japan, and it grows wild in the South. It is grown by gardeners who admire the smooth stalks and graceful leaves. Some people make furniture out of bamboo, while others even create houses made of bamboo. One of the most popular new forms of flooring is bamboo because it is considered environmentally friendly. Bamboo grows quickly, so it quickly replaces itself, unlike most other kinds of building lumber. Nonetheless, it can overpower other plants in an area.

Name _____ Date _____

CHAPTER 16   Adverbial Clauses

[16B.1] An **adverbial clause** is a subordinate clause that is used as an adverb to modify a verb, an adjective, or an adverb.

> **EXERCISE** Choose the word or words the underlined adverbial clause modifies.

_____ 1. Clara finished the assignment <u>faster than I did</u>.
  A finished
  B assignment

_____ 2. <u>If you drive tomorrow</u>, I will drive tonight.
  A will drive
  B tonight

_____ 3. A date palm cannot grow <u>unless its roots are in water</u>.
  A palm
  B cannot grow

_____ 4. An ostrich can run faster <u>than any other bird does</u>.
  A ostrich
  B faster

_____ 5. The beaches of Bermuda are pink <u>because rose-colored shells wash ashore</u>.
  A are
  B pink

_____ 6. <u>After Cortez reached Mexico City</u>, he was met by Montezuma.
  A was met
  B Montezuma

_____ 7. <u>When porpoises are trained</u>, they can play basketball.
  A can play
  B basketball

_____ 8. The Pacific Ocean is larger <u>than the Atlantic Ocean</u>.
  A is
  B larger

_____ 9. The sun sets earlier <u>when winter arrives</u>.
  A sets
  B earlier

_____ 10. I listen to the weather report <u>before I get dressed</u>.
  A listen
  B report

_____ 11. <u>Since the bus was late</u>, I walked home.
  A I
  B walked

_____ 12. <u>Since falcons usually live on cliff tops</u>, they adjust well to living on tall buildings.
  A adjust
  B living

CHAPTER 16 Adverbial Clauses

EXERCISE A Underline the adverbial clause in the following sentences. Write the word or words the adverbial clause modifies on the line.

_____ 1. Whenever the sun shines, people seem more cheerful.

_____ 2. As I have just learned, rats are fairly intelligent.

_____ 3. Before he became a pirate, Captain Kidd lived in New York.

_____ 4. When a jackrabbit jumps, it can cover fifteen feet at a time.

_____ 5. Maria gets good grades more often than Tina does.

_____ 6. Even though we fertilized it, the lawn turned brown.

_____ 7. While it hibernates, a polar bear can live without food.

_____ 8. The daffodils bloomed later this spring than they did last year.

_____ 9. Because you were tired, you made more mistakes.

_____ 10. After it was charged with neglect, the parks department hired more landscaping workers.

EXERCISE B Add information to expand the following adverbial clauses into complete sentences. Remember to use correct capitalization and punctuation.

11. Even though Rick hasn't been to China, _____

_____

12. When it is noon in Boston, _____

_____

13. When they are tired, _____

_____

14. _____ than we thought.

15. While they soar overhead at dusk, _____

_____

Name _____ Date _____

CHAPTER 16 — Punctuation with Adverbial Clauses

EXERCISE A Underline the adverbial clauses in the following paragraph. Add commas where needed.

Before cutting tools were made of copper and bronze they were made of flint. Because it could be shaped easily flint was more practical to use than stone. Early people used sharp flint knives and spears when they hunted. Even though metal knives can be purchased anywhere some craftsmen still enjoy making knives from flint. Flintnapping is a challenging hobby because it can take a year or more to become skilled enough to fashion a usable spear or knife.

EXERCISE B Underline the adverbial clause in each sentence. Then write I if the adverbial clause is punctuated incorrectly, or C if it is punctuated correctly. If the adverbial clause is punctuated incorrectly, correct it by adding any necessary commas or crossing out unnecessary ones.

_____ 1. When a starfish captures an oyster the starfish wraps its arms around the oyster.

_____ 2. Even though the sea anemone looks like a flower, it is a flesh-eating animal.

_____ 3. This flower, if it needs to can move along the ocean bottom.

_____ 4. Because it is covered with sharp spines the sea urchin looks like a pincushion.

_____ 5. Its spines protect it when it is attacked.

_____ 6. The tail of a sea horse, when the sea horse wraps it around a piece of seaweed becomes a handy anchor.

_____ 7. The sea horse, because it looks like a tiny horse is well named.

_____ 8. Humpback whales feed at the surface when they are hungry.

Name _____ Date _____

CHAPTER 16 Elliptical Clauses

[16B.2] An adverbial clause in which words are missing is called an **elliptical clause**.

EXERCISE A Choose the word or words that best complete the underlined elliptical clause in each sentence.

_____ 1. Francis is taller <u>than I</u>.
    A am
    B am tall

_____ 2. Not many other birds fly <u>as fast as hawks</u>.
    A fly
    B fast

_____ 3. Bob spends more time on the courts <u>than Ted</u>.
    A spends
    B has

_____ 4. Jupiter is two-and-a-half times larger <u>than any other planet</u>.
    A is
    B grows

_____ 5. A badminton court is not <u>as large as a tennis court</u>.
    A weighs
    B is

_____ 6. A brown bear is less dangerous <u>than a grizzly bear</u>.
    A is
    B is less dangerous

EXERCISE B Write the completed version of each elliptical clause in the following sentences.

7. Do you really believe that Alicia would be a more effective chairperson than he _____

8. Except when my mother wears high heels, she is shorter than I _____

9. I think Bud plays the cello better than I _____

10. Who can run as fast and as far as I _____

11. Those four peaches look riper than the others _____

12. Coal is made of the same chemical element as diamonds _____

CHAPTER 16 Adjectival Clauses

[16B.3] An **adjectival clause** is a subordinate clause that is used as an adjective to modify a noun or a pronoun.

EXERCISE A Choose the word the underlined adjectival clause modifies in each sentence.

_____ 1. The host who entertains a friend is happy.
   A host
   B happy

_____ 2. One kind of spider in Australia makes a web that people use as a fishing net.
   A spider
   B web

_____ 3. The sea turtle is one sea animal that lays its eggs on shore.
   A turtle
   B animal

_____ 4. Curling is a sport that is popular in Canada.
   A Curling
   B sport

_____ 5. Root vegetables are ones that keep well without refrigeration.
   A vegetables
   B ones

_____ 6. One who is eighteen is entitled to vote.
   A One
   B vote

EXERCISE B Underline the adjectival clause in the following sentences. Draw an arrow to the word or words the clause modifies.

7. There is a type of mushroom that can live for fifty years.

8. The plumber fixed the leaky faucet that had been dripping all day.

9. The waitress swept up the pieces of the plate that fell and shattered.

10. The chenille sweater, which was a gift from Alice's grandmother, was lost.

11. You should eat leafy spinach, which is green and nutritious.

12. My karate instructor, who believes in self-discipline, meditates an hour a day.

13. The first dictionaries, which consisted of rare, difficult, or specialized words, were produced by ancient Greeks and Romans.

14. Babe Didrikson, who was an outstanding golfer, runner, and basketball player, was one of the greatest athletes in history.

CHAPTER 16 Relative Pronouns in Adjectival Clauses

[16B.4] A **relative pronoun** relates an adjectival clause to its antecedent—the noun or pronoun the clause modifies. Within the adjectival clause, the relative pronoun can function as a subject, a direct object, or an object of a preposition. It may also show possession.

EXERCISE For each sentence, underline the adjectival clause and circle the relative pronoun. Then choose the function of the relative pronoun in the underlined adjectival clause.

_____ 1. Otters are animals that play a lot.
  A subject
  B direct object
  C object of a preposition
  D possession

_____ 2. An Eskimo kayak is a boat in which only one person rides.
  A subject
  B direct object
  C object of a preposition
  D possession

_____ 3. That is an idea whose time has come.
  A subject
  B direct object
  C object of a preposition
  D possession

_____ 4. Computer games provide tests of quick thinking that I find challenging.
  A subject
  B direct object
  C object of a preposition
  D possession

_____ 5. Charlie is the man who gives the weather report every evening.
  A subject
  B direct object
  C object of a preposition
  D possession

_____ 6. This is the plant that I grew under lights.
  A subject
  B direct object
  C object of a preposition
  D possession

_____ 7. Chang is the player for whom I always cheer.
  A subject
  B direct object
  C object of a preposition
  D possession

_____ 8. Michael Jackson was a singer whose voice is familiar to millions.
  A subject
  B direct object
  C object of a preposition
  D possession

_____ 9. Colds consist of various symptoms that affect people differently.
  A subject
  B direct object
  C object of a preposition
  D possession

_____ 10. It was an American who popularized crossword puzzles.
  A subject
  B direct object
  C object of a preposition
  D possession

CHAPTER 16 Punctuation with Adjectival Clauses

EXERCISE A Choose the sentence in which the adjectival clause is correctly punctuated.

_____ 1. **A** An aerial tram, which goes straight up a mountain, is used by skiers.
B An aerial tram which goes straight up a mountain is used by skiers.

_____ 2. **A** Queen Elizabeth I, who knighted Sir Francis Drake, lived at the same time as William Shakespeare.
B Queen Elizabeth I who knighted Sir Francis Drake lived at the same time as William Shakespeare.

_____ 3. **A** The plane, that will leave for Maine, has fan-jet engines.
B The plane that will leave for Maine has fan-jet engines.

_____ 4. **A** The deserts, that cover North Africa, are increasing in size.
B The deserts that cover North Africa are increasing in size.

_____ 5. **A** Lake Louise, which is at the foot of Victoria Glacier, is milky in color.
B Lake Louise which is at the foot of Victoria Glacier is milky in color.

_____ 6. **A** Onions, which are members of the lily family, grow in all fifty states.
B Onions which are members of the lily family grow in all fifty states.

EXERCISE B Underline each adjectival clause. Write I if the adjectival clause is punctuated incorrectly, and C if it is punctuated correctly. If it is punctuated incorrectly, correct it by adding any necessary commas or crossing out unnecessary ones.

_____ 7. Corn which cannot disperse its own seeds, dies without human care.

_____ 8. People, who become Olympic stars, are dedicated athletes.

_____ 9. The man who built the first submarine in 1620 covered it with leather.

_____ 10. Isaac Asimov who writes science fiction sometimes writes under the name Paul French.

_____ 11. Jerry belongs to a computer club, that meets Tuesdays after school.

_____ 12. The photographer who took the first aerial photograph, was in a balloon.

_____ 13. Lewis Carroll, who wrote *Alice's Adventures in Wonderland* wrote 98,721 letters over 37 years.

_____ 14. Female polar bears, that are going to have cubs, look for ice caves.

_____ 15. He still uses snail mail which adds another week to the processing time.

CHAPTER 16 — Misplaced Modifiers

EXERCISE A Underline the adjectival clause in each sentence. Write MM for misplaced modifier if the underlined clause is used incorrectly. Write C for correct if the underlined modifier is used correctly.

_____ 1. Lynn returned the sweater that she had planned to wear on the trip to the store.

_____ 2. A pizza appeared on the table that was covered with cheese.

_____ 3. Jim put his essay, on which he had slaved, on the teacher's desk.

_____ 4. Barbara downloaded the information that she found in the encyclopedia onto her computer.

_____ 5. We rented a cottage at the lake that had two rooms.

_____ 6. Glenn rode to the market in the bus where he buys his groceries.

_____ 7. The doctor walked into the room who was carrying the stethoscope.

_____ 8. The patient described the ailments that had plagued her for three days.

_____ 9. The doctor prescribed a mild pain reliever, which could be purchased at a pharmacy.

_____ 10. Dr. Burke, who felt better already, advised her patient to drink milk with the medicine.

EXERCISE B Rewrite the incorrect sentences from the preceding exercise, correcting each misplaced modifier. Use a comma or commas where needed.

CHAPTER 16 — Noun Clauses

[16B.5] A **noun clause** is a subordinate clause that is used as a noun.

EXERCISE Underline the noun clause in each sentence.

1. A club is to a golfer <u>what a bat is to a baseball player</u>.

2. Did you know <u>that only female mosquitoes bite</u>?

3. Give <u>whomever you like</u> the extra pair of tickets.

4. Do you know <u>who invented carbonated drinks</u>?

5. Sell the bike for <u>whatever price seems reasonable</u>.

6. <u>What you eat</u> will affect your health.

7. <u>That crossword puzzles are popular</u> is certainly true.

8. A thermometer is <u>what we need now</u>.

9. <u>Whose shirt this is</u> is a mystery.

10. Send <u>whomever wins the race</u> this surprise gift.

11. That is <u>why I am studying science</u>.

12. <u>That chalk is composed of fossil shells</u> surprises me.

13. <u>That she would not tell anyone</u> is unthinkable.

14. <u>Whoever drove the car</u> did not turn off the lights.

15. Hand the paper to <u>whomever wrote it</u>.

CHAPTER 16 Noun Clauses

EXERCISE Underline the noun clause in each sentence. Then select how the underlined noun clause is used.

_____ 1. Can you explain <u>how butter is made</u>?
   A subject
   B direct object
   C indirect object
   D object of the preposition
   E predicate nominative

_____ 2. Give <u>whomever answers the phone</u> the message.
   A subject
   B direct object
   C indirect object
   D object of the preposition
   E predicate nominative

_____ 3. <u>What she did on water skis</u> was difficult.
   A subject
   B direct object
   C indirect object
   D object of the preposition
   E predicate nominative

_____ 4. We will leave at <u>whatever hour you suggest</u>.
   A subject
   B direct object
   C indirect object
   D object of the preposition
   E predicate nominative

_____ 5. A glass of water is <u>what I want most</u>.
   A subject
   B direct object
   C indirect object
   D object of the preposition
   E predicate nominative

_____ 6. Do you believe <u>that life exists in outer space</u>?
   A subject
   B direct object
   C indirect object
   D object of the preposition
   E predicate nominative

_____ 7. Bring <u>whatever you like</u> to the party.
   A subject
   B direct object
   C indirect object
   D object of the preposition
   E predicate nominative

_____ 8. The announcer says <u>that rain is expected</u>.
   A subject
   B direct object
   C indirect object
   D object of the preposition
   E predicate nominative

_____ 9. <u>What we need</u> is better public transportation.
   A subject
   B direct object
   C indirect object
   D object of the preposition
   E predicate nominative

_____ 10. Have you thought about <u>what you will do this summer</u>?
   A subject
   B direct object
   C indirect object
   D object of the preposition
   E predicate nominative

Name _____ Date _____

CHAPTER 16 Adverbial, Adjectival, and Noun Clauses

EXERCISE A Write the letter of the term that correctly identifies each sentence or underlined part of a sentence.

_____ 1. Municipal corporations may be created by <u>whomever wants to administer a town or village</u>.
  A adverbial clause **B** adjectival clause **C** noun clause

_____ 2. There are even ecclesiastical corporations, <u>which are created for religious purposes</u>.
  A adverbial clause **B** adjectival clause **C** noun clause

_____ 3. <u>If you started a corporation all by yourself</u>, it would be called a sole corporation.
  A adverbial clause **B** adjectival clause **C** noun clause

_____ 4. You may start a corporation <u>even though you work alone in your basement</u>.
  A adverbial clause **B** adjectival clause **C** noun clause

_____ 5. <u>Whatever you produce</u> can be a valuable commodity.
  A adverbial clause **B** adjectival clause **C** noun clause

_____ 6. A nonprofit organization is a group <u>that does not distribute its surplus funds to shareholders</u>.
  A adverbial clause **B** adjectival clause **C** noun clause

_____ 7. It is true <u>that many nonprofit organizations are charities</u>.
  A adverbial clause **B** adjectival clause **C** noun clause

EXERCISE B Write a sentence that follows each direction. Include commas where needed.

8. Include an adverbial clause that begins with *because*.
   _____
   _____

9. Include an adjectival clause at the end of the sentence.
   _____
   _____

10. Include a noun clause that is used as a subject.
    _____
    _____

11. Include a noun clause that is used as a direct object.
    _____
    _____

Name _____ Date _____

CHAPTER 16 — Kinds of Sentence Structure

[16C.1] A **simple sentence** consists of one independent clause.
[16C.2] A **compound sentence** consists of two or more independent clauses.
[16C.3] A **complex sentence** consists of one independent clause and one or more subordinate clauses.
[16C.4] A **compound-complex sentence** consists of two or more independent clauses and one or more subordinate clauses.

> **EXERCISE** For the following sentences, underline each independent clause once and each subordinate clause twice. Then choose whether each sentence is a simple sentence, compound sentence, complex sentence, or compound-complex sentence.

_____ 1. Almost anything that you can pick up is collectible.
  A simple sentence
  B compound sentence
  C complex sentence
  D compound-complex sentence

_____ 2. Some people collect stamps, and others collect shells.
  A simple sentence
  B compound sentence
  C complex sentence
  D compound-complex sentence

_____ 3. Gum wrappers are collectors' items, and buttons are too.
  A simple sentence
  B compound sentence
  C complex sentence
  D compound-complex sentence

_____ 4. Old postcards can sometimes have value.
  A simple sentence
  B compound sentence
  C complex sentence
  D compound-complex sentence

_____ 5. They are often located in old trunks or in secondhand stores.
  A simple sentence
  B compound sentence
  C complex sentence
  D compound-complex sentence

_____ 6. Old postcards that advertise a product are particularly valuable.
  A simple sentence
  B compound sentence
  C complex sentence
  D compound-complex sentence

_____ 7. Some collect cards for their value, but others collect them because they like the pictures on them.
  A simple sentence
  B compound sentence
  C complex sentence
  D compound-complex sentence

_____ 8. Autographs are a favorite collector's item, and some stores specialize in the sale of them.
  A simple sentence
  B compound sentence
  C complex sentence
  D compound-complex sentence

_____ 9. Autographs of the famous can be valuable.
  A simple sentence
  B compound sentence
  C complex sentence
  D compound-complex sentence

_____ 10. Some autographs do not become valuable until years have passed.
  A simple sentence
  B compound sentence
  C complex sentence
  D compound-complex sentence

CHAPTER 16   Clause Fragments

[16D] A subordinate clause becomes a **clause fragment** if it stands alone.

EXERCISE A Write S if the following is a complete sentence or F it is a clause fragment.

_____ 1. Where the water lilies cannot grow on the surface.

_____ 2. That you want to be a big brother is admirable.

_____ 3. Although the king wasn't elected.

_____ 4. Where I am is where I want to be.

_____ 5. Since the time isn't right and I haven't received an allowance.

_____ 6. Natasha is a famous yoga instructor.

_____ 7. William wants to go to graduate school after college.

_____ 8. After the time I thought my shoe was lost in the mud.

_____ 9. The man behind the counter thought I was famous.

_____ 10. When it was time, we stepped onto the stage.

EXERCISE B Use each fragment in the preceding exercise in a complete sentence. Add capital letters and punctuation where needed.

CHAPTER 16 Run-on Sentences

[16E] A **run-on sentence** is two or more sentences written as one sentence and separated by a comma or no mark of punctuation at all.

EXERCISE Rewrite the following paragraphs, correcting any run-on sentences.

The Amazon rain forest occupies about 2.5 million square miles, it accounts for about one-half of the world's remaining rain forest. Not all the rain forests in the world are in the Amazon about twenty percent of rain forests that remain in the world are in Africa. Another twenty-five percent of the world's remaining rain forests are in Southeast Asia they are divided up among the many islands of the region. Papua New Guinea, Australia, Malaysia, and the Philippines are other countries that contain sizable rain forests.

I traveled to the Amazon rain forest with a school group and saw areas that had been cleared by farmers, the farmers clear small plots of land to grow their crops. I met a farmer who made a humble living making charcoal and selling it at a market, he had to travel two days on the river to go to the market. The farmer made charcoal from the trees that he cut down on his plot of land, he also grew casava to sell at the market. The people who live in the rain forest have to farm in order to feed their families.

CHAPTER 16 Fragments and Run-on Sentences

EXERCISE On the lines below, rewrite the following passage, correcting any sentence fragments or run-on sentences. Be sure to use correct punctuation.

The situation in the Amazon rain forest is a very serious problem there is no easy solution. In many Central American countries. Enormous plantations have acquired most of the fertile farming land, the family farmers have no choice but to cut new plots of land out of the rain forest, where the soil is less fertile. Scientists say that the diversity of the rain forest is of great benefit to humans. Many of the animals, plants, fungi, and bacteria. That exist in the rain forest are useful to humans, we get food, medicines, and other products from them. Many believe that the rain forest is home to more than one-third of all living species on Earth most of them remain unknown or not described. The degradation of the rain forest must stop it is just as important as the United States and other countries having a source of cheap food to import.

Name _____ Date _____

CHAPTER 16 — Clauses Review

EXERCISE Read the paragraph and answer the questions that follow.

> Scientists report **(1)** <u>that creatures living in the deep sea are in danger of starving to death</u>. Millions of undiscovered species live, in the deep sea. Creatures in the seabed are suffering from growing food shortages. Which may be a result of rising sea temperatures. Scientists believe that some species will die out, those that can survive on a low food supply will continue living. Not much is known about the creatures that live in the deep sea, not much is known about the changes in their diets. Scientists estimate that up to 10 million species live in the depths of the sea. Most animals of the deep rely on food chains that begin. In the lighted realms of the sea. Microscopic plants called phytoplankton. Capture the sun and start the food cycle. **(2)** <u>Wherever there are animal droppings</u>, there is a constant rain of organic matter **(3)** <u>that feeds the bottom dwellers</u>.

_____ 1. The underlined part of sentence 1 is what kind of clause?

    A adverbial clause   **B** adjectival clause   **C** noun clause

_____ 2. The underlined part of sentence 2 is what kind of clause?

    A adverbial clause   **B** adjectival clause   **C** noun clause

_____ 3. The underlined part of sentence 3 is what kind of clause?

    A adverbial clause   **B** adjectival clause   **C** noun clause

4. Rewrite the paragraph above, correcting any fragments and run-on sentences. Be sure to use correct punctuation.

_____
_____
_____
_____
_____
_____
_____
_____
_____
_____
_____
_____

Name _____ Date _____

CHAPTER 17 — Principal Parts of Irregular Verbs

[17A] The **principal parts** of a verb are the present, the present participle, the past, and the past participle.

[17A.2] An **irregular verb** does not form its past and past participle by adding *-ed* or *-d* to the present.

EXERCISE A Choose the correct form of the past or past participle of each verb in parentheses.

_____ 1. All of the children have (lose) their baby teeth.
  A lost
  B losed
  C loss

_____ 2. Three American swimmers (win) gold medals.
  A win
  B winned
  C won

_____ 3. The United States has (send) thousands of objects into space.
  A sent
  B sends
  C sending

_____ 4. Frank (lay) the paint can on the porch steps.
  A lay
  B lain
  C laid

_____ 5. Many people have (find) fossilized dinosaur footprints along the Connecticut River.
  A finds
  B found
  C finded

_____ 6. These DVDs (cost) very little at the sale.
  A costed
  B cost
  C costing

_____ 7. Many immigrants have (bring) their customs to this country.
  A brought
  B bringed
  C brung

EXERCISE B Choose the accurate form of the past or past participle of each underlined verb. If the verb is correct, choose *No error* as the answer.

_____ 8. We <u>sell</u> dozens of magazine subscriptions last week.
  A selled
  B sold
  C No error

_____ 9. Surprisingly, they have <u>keep</u> the secret to themselves.
  A kept
  B keeping
  C No error

_____ 10. The United States has <u>lead</u> the field in the development of computers.
  A leads
  B led
  C No error

_____ 11. After dinner everyone <u>sit</u> down in the shade of the big oak tree.
  A sits
  B sat
  C No error

continued

Chapter 17: Principal Parts of Irregular Verbs continued

_____ 12. Bill has <u>set</u> the alarm for five o'clock.
  - **A** sets
  - **B** setted
  - **C** No error

_____ 13. Many visitors have <u>lose</u> their way in this city.
  - **A** lost
  - **B** losed
  - **C** No error

_____ 14. The spider has <u>catch</u> a beetle in her web.
  - **A** catched
  - **B** caught
  - **C** No error

_____ 15. Patsy <u>write</u> a birthday card to her Peruvian pen pal.
  - **A** writes
  - **B** wrote
  - **C** No error

_____ 16. For many years the Chinese have <u>buy</u> grain from the United States.
  - **A** bought
  - **B** buying
  - **C** No error

_____ 17. Who knows how long she has <u>feel</u> that way?
  - **A** felt
  - **B** feeling
  - **C** No error

Name _____ Date _____

CHAPTER 17 — Principal Parts of Irregular Verbs

EXERCISE A Underline the main verb in each sentence. Then choose the correct form of the irregular verb as past (P), present participle (PP), or past participle (Past P).

_____ 1. Claude is getting a new computer for his birthday this year.

_____ 2. Yes, I have chosen Wanda as winner of the essay contest.

_____ 3. Miranda did the crossword puzzle in only ten minutes.

_____ 4. The girls have shown their report cards to their parents.

_____ 5. Keisha told her mother about the terrible accident.

_____ 6. I am seeing more clearly now with my new glasses.

_____ 7. Mrs. Miller has dealt the cards for the next round of canasta.

_____ 8. Who has swum the fastest backstroke in this year's meet?

_____ 9. Her favorite shirt shrank in the washing machine.

_____ 10. Lee has bound the twigs with heavy twine.

EXERCISE B In the blank provided, write the correct form of the past or the past participle of each verb in parentheses.

_____ 11. The ice cubes (freeze) quickly in the freezer compartment.

_____ 12. The Democratic party has not (choose) its slate of candidates.

_____ 13. The runner (steal) second base, and the crowd roared.

_____ 14. At the rally the candidates (speak) about most of the issues.

_____ 15. Many mountain climbers have (freeze) their fingers and toes.

_____ 16. A. J. Foyt (break) all records at the Indianapolis 500 race.

_____ 17. The tennis team (fly) to Miami for the tournament.

_____ 18. The author has recently (wrote) her fifteenth novel.

_____ 19. (Be) you in the room when he quit?

_____ 20. It doesn't matter if you have (see) it before, you're going to watch it again.

Name _____ Date _____

CHAPTER 17 — Verb Tense

[17C] The time expressed by a verb is called the **tense** of a verb. Six basic tenses—three simple tenses and three perfect tenses—show whether something is happening now, has happened in the past, or will happen in the future.

EXERCISE A Choose the correct tense of each underlined verb.

_____ 1. Luther Burbank <u>developed</u> more than 800 new plant varieties.
  A present
  B past
  C future

_____ 2. All of these flowers <u>will produce</u> seeds in the fall.
  A present
  B past
  C future

_____ 3. The climate of Florida <u>favors</u> the growth of citrus fruit.
  A present
  B past
  C future

_____ 4. Eric the Red <u>named</u> a land of eternal ice and snow Greenland.
  A present
  B past
  C future

_____ 5. Columbus never <u>reached</u> what is now the United States.
  A present
  B past
  C future

_____ 6. Standard time <u>will return</u> at the end of October.
  A present
  B past
  C future

EXERCISE B Underline the main verb and label it as *present*, *past*, or *future*.

_____ 7. The storm will hit the Gulf Coast tomorrow afternoon.

_____ 8. The Mesozoic Era gave birth to flying reptiles.

_____ 9. The moon is the closest celestial body to Earth.

_____ 10. April showers will bring May flowers.

_____ 11. A cumulus cloud resembles a giant white cotton ball.

_____ 12. Igor Stravinsky composed the epochal ballet *The Firebird*.

_____ 13. In 1907, Guglielmo Marconi secured a patent for his radio.

Name _____ Date _____

CHAPTER 17 Verb Tense

EXERCISE A Choose the correct tense of each underlined verb.

_____ 1. I have seen many catfish in this pond.
   A present perfect
   B past perfect
   C future perfect

_____ 2. The crew will have paved this street by Tuesday.
   A present perfect
   B past perfect
   C future perfect

_____ 3. We had arrived before the alarm went off.
   A present perfect
   B past perfect
   C future perfect

_____ 4. Perhaps a lack of water has stunted the growth of these plants.
   A present perfect
   B past perfect
   C future perfect

_____ 5. They will have eaten supper with us twice this week.
   A present perfect
   B past perfect
   C future perfect

_____ 6. Most of the buildings had been torn down after the World's Fair.
   A present perfect
   B past perfect
   C future perfect

EXERCISE B Underline the correct form of the verb in parentheses.

7. Edgar suddenly realized he (forgot, had forgotten) to buy eggs at the store.

8. He remembered as soon as he (opens, opened) the refrigerator door.

9. He (was, had been) glad his mother was not yet home.

10. After quickly putting the other groceries away, he (ran, runs) back to the supermarket.

11. The dairy aisle (displayed, had displayed) rows of milk and cheese but no eggs.

12. He (looked, will have looked) incredulously at the dairy aisle.

13. For the past two weeks, the manager explained, the egg shipments (would arrive, had arrived) at the end of the day.

14. Edgar thought he (had seen, will see) some eggs in a quick carry-out case in front of the store.

15. The manager told him he never (put, had put) eggs there—only milk.

16. When Edgar checked up front, he (will find, found) he was right—there were indeed some cartons of eggs, next to the other quick carry-out items.

CHAPTER 17 — Uses of the Tenses

EXERCISE Choose the correct form of the verb in parentheses and write it on the line provided. Some answers may vary.

_____ 1. The race (finish) by the time we get to the starting line.

_____ 2. Through the still night air (come) the hoot of the diesel engine.

_____ 3. Yesterday Christine (take) her first guitar lesson.

_____ 4. Mr. Lampkin informed me that he (enter) my sculpture in the competition.

_____ 5. For weeks now Don (practice) his fast ball.

_____ 6. This year I (wear) out two pairs of sneakers.

_____ 7. In the Olympics this year, Patti (win) a gold medal.

_____ 8. Now Gail (want) her turn on the pitcher's mound.

_____ 9. Jack (take) the clock apart and was now cleaning and oiling it.

_____ 10. When Thomas Edison was thirty-one, he (invent) the phonograph.

_____ 11. Yesterday we (pick) a pint of raspberries from our bushes.

_____ 12. By the time Dottie got there, the show (begin).

_____ 13. Before Peggy realized what (happen), she was following her dance partner perfectly.

_____ 14. When Terry was a freshman, he (learn) step dancing.

_____ 15. For two years now, I (take) computer programming.

CHAPTER 17 Uses of the Tenses

EXERCISE Complete the sentence by choosing the correct form of the verb shown in parentheses.

_____ 1. Silas Marner remembered that he (give) his knife to William Dane.
  A had given
  B gave
  C will have given

_____ 2. When Paul and Brian reached the summit, they (flop) down immediately on the ledge.
  A flopped
  B were flopping
  C had flopped

_____ 3. Nick (take) the spools out of the typewriter, and now he is trying to put in a new ribbon.
  A has taken
  B had taken
  C takes

_____ 4. Renée telephoned to say that she (send) the keys to Greta.
  A sent
  B had sent
  C will have sent

_____ 5. When I saw the empty plate, I asked who (eat) all the sandwiches.
  A had eaten
  B are eating
  C ate

_____ 6. So far, ninety girls (report) for practice on the basketball team.
  A reported
  B will have reported
  C have reported

_____ 7. Suddenly Dean began to regret that he (volunteer) for state crew.
  A will volunteer
  B volunteered
  C had volunteered

_____ 8. So far this winter, I (go) skiing nine times.
  A will have gone
  B have gone
  C went

_____ 9. Of course everyone who will listen to Gina sing (applaud).
  A applauds
  B will have applauded
  C will applaud

_____ 10. If Bess (wear) her wet suit, she could have stayed in the water longer.
  A wore
  B had worn
  C has been wearing

_____ 11. I am happy that Debbie (win) three bowling tournaments this year.
  A has won
  B will win
  C is winning

_____ 12. The elephant filled its trunk with water and (give) itself a cool shower.
  A gave
  B will have given
  C had given

_____ 13. Dale measured the bamboo every day to see how much it (grow).
  A grows
  B grew
  C had grown

_____ 14. If Betsy (play) her music a little more softly, her grandmother would still be asleep.
  A played
  B had played
  C plays

CHAPTER 17 — Progressive and Emphatic Forms

[17D.3] The **progressive forms** are used to express continuing or ongoing action. To write the progressive forms, add a present or perfect tense of the verb *be* to the present participle.

[17D.4] The **emphatic forms** of the present and past tense of verbs are mainly used to show emphasis or force. To write the present emphatic, add *do* or *does* to the present tense of a verb. To write the past emphatic, add *did* to the present tense.

EXERCISE Underline the verb phrase. Choose the progressive or emphatic verb tense that is used in each sentence.

_____ 1. Lightning was flashing in the distance.
  A present progressive
  B past progressive
  C past perfect progressive

_____ 2. By Friday the couple will have been dancing for a record six days.
  A future perfect progressive
  B present perfect progressive
  C future progressive

_____ 3. Right now the mechanic is repairing a dune buggy.
  A future progressive
  B past progressive
  C present progressive

_____ 4. The Cougars had been winning until the third quarter of the game.
  A present perfect progressive
  B past perfect progressive
  C past progressive

_____ 5. The horses did seem a little skittish yesterday.
  A past progressive
  B past emphatic
  C present emphatic

_____ 6. Lizzie will be attending the concert tomorrow.
  A present progressive
  B future progressive
  C future perfect progressive

_____ 7. The famous trumpet player is performing at the holiday concert.
  A present progressive
  B future progressive
  C present perfect progressive

_____ 8. The library does offer a wide range of programs throughout the year.
  A present emphatic
  B past progressive
  C past emphatic

_____ 9. Ms. Palmer has been organizing the class schedules for us.
  A present perfect progressive
  B past progressive
  C present progressive

_____ 10. We had been listening to the radio when the lights went out.
  A present perfect progressive
  B past progressive
  C past perfect progressive

_____ 11. Kalman had been sleeping throughout that memorable day.
  A future perfect progressive
  B past perfect progressive
  C present perfect progressive

_____ 12. Sammi will have been writing her novel for two years this week.
  A present progressive
  B future progressive
  C future perfect progressive

_____ 13. The candidates for homecoming queen will be hearing the final results tonight.
  A future progressive
  B future perfect progressive
  C present progressive

CHAPTER 17 Shifts in Tense

EXERCISE Using the base form of the verb in parentheses, write the correct verb form for each sentence.

_____ 1. At the restaurant I had spaghetti, but my brother (eat) only a small salad.

_____ 2. She started the blender, and the bananas (become) mush.

_____ 3. I looked everywhere in the house, and I finally (find) the missing ring.

_____ 4. While the dog slept on the porch, the kitten (climb) on top of his head.

_____ 5. I understand that you (leave) the firm next month.

_____ 6. We will be planning the party events tomorrow; we (hire) the magician as well.

_____ 7. The shortstop began to throw the ball and then suddenly (drop) it.

_____ 8. Today golf is more popular than it (be) in the past.

_____ 9. Steven received a gift from Jill, who (include) a card inside the package.

_____ 10. Ethan hurt his finger when he (slide) into third base.

_____ 11. We found no pennies in the jar, but there (be) many nickels.

_____ 12. Ann will visit colleges next week, and then in a month she (make) a decision.

_____ 13. By tomorrow, I will have cleaned the house, and Sam (paint) the doors.

_____ 14. Three sparrows are living in our attic, and a mouse (scamper) around our basement.

_____ 15. For last year's animal art contest, Gil had sculpted an alligator, and Martha (draw) a flock of geese.

Name _____ Date _____

CHAPTER 17 Using Correct Verb Forms

EXERCISE A Cross out any incorrect verbs and write the correct form in the blank. If the verb form is correct, write C.

_____ 1. These officials believed that the slaves had stole their freedom.

_____ 2. The captors often selled the slaves back to their owners.

_____ 3. Sometimes the fear of horrible punishment kept the slaves from escaping.

_____ 4. Harriet Tubman leaded hundreds of slaves to freedom.

_____ 5. Tubman breaked away from her owners in Maryland.

_____ 6. She put on disguises for most of her trips back to the South.

_____ 7. Some people saying she was like Moses.

_____ 8. Many slaves still losed their lives, searching for freedom.

_____ 9. Our family drived along a probable Underground Railroad route.

_____ 10. Along the way my mother spoke to us about the injustice of slavery.

EXERCISE B Complete each pair of sentences by supplying the correct forms of the verb in parentheses.

_____ 11. (eat) Who _____ my appetizers? I had _____ only one bite.

_____ 12. (drink) Have you ever _____ punch like this? Yes, I _____ some at the homecoming dance.

_____ 13. (go) Have you _____ to prom before? I _____ last year as a sophomore.

_____ 14. (write) I _____ about the prom for the yearbook. Have you _____ for the yearbook?

_____ 15. (swim) Have you ever _____ in a river? No, but I _____ in the ocean once.

Name _____ Date _____

CHAPTER 17 Active and Passive Voice

[17E] The **active voice** indicates that the subject is performing the action. The **passive voice** indicates that the action of the verb is being performed upon the subject.

EXERCISE A Underline any verbs or verb phrases that are in the passive voice.

All states have a lawmaking body. This is called a legislature or general assembly. The legislature or general assembly is usually divided into two houses, although Nebraska is governed via a unicameral form of government. In most states the upper house is called the Senate. The lower house is known as the House of Representatives. State senators are elected every four years. The people elect representatives or assembly members every two years. Many state legislatures meet biennially, although some are called back to business when there are pressing economic or political issues.

EXERCISE B Underline each verb phrase (all are in the passive voice). Write I if the use of passive voice is inappropriate and A if its use is appropriate.

_____ 1. Modern marionettes are operated by strings.

_____ 2. Plenty of seats were made available for the whole audience.

_____ 3. De Rozier's balloon was nearly wrecked by a strong gust of wind.

_____ 4. The locomotive DeWitt Clinton was named for a governor of New York.

_____ 5. The picture was drawn by Mae Beth on the whiteboard.

_____ 6. My jacket was found on the steps by Jim.

_____ 7. Daylight saving time is attained by advancing the clock one hour.

_____ 8. In 1967, the Uniform Time Act was put into effect in the United States.

_____ 9. Daylight saving time was extended to conserve energy.

_____ 10. Throughout the world, clock time is adjusted for added daylight in the summer.

Name _____ Date _____

CHAPTER 17 Mood

[17F] The **mood** of a verb is the way in which a verb expresses an idea.
[17F.1] The **indicative mood** is used to state a fact or to ask a question.
[17F.2] The **imperative mood** is used to give a command or to make a request.
[17F.3] The **subjunctive mood** is used to express a condition contrary to fact that begins with words such as *if, as if,* or *as though*. It is also use to express a wish, command, or a request after the word *that*.

EXERCISE Choose the letter that indicates the mood of the sentence.

_____ 1. I wish I were on the skiing team again this year.
    A indicative
    B imperative
    C subjunctive

_____ 2. Ned looks as if he were on his last legs.
    A indicative
    B imperative
    C subjunctive

_____ 3. Mona climbed to the top of the Washington Monument last year.
    A indicative
    B imperative
    C subjunctive

_____ 4. If I were you, I'd send for a sporting goods catalog.
    A indicative
    B imperative
    C subjunctive

_____ 5. Pass the suntan lotion, Jeff.
    A indicative
    B imperative
    C subjunctive

_____ 6. Did Gerry really swim across the lake?
    A indicative
    B imperative
    C subjunctive

_____ 7. You talk as though Mark were the only player on the entire field.
    A indicative
    B imperative
    C subjunctive

EXERCISE B Underline the correct form of the verb in parentheses.

8. The lunchroom staff suggested that they (are, be) given a raise.
9. I wish I (was, were) going to graduate a year early.
10. If she (was, were) taller, she would have a better shot at making the varsity team.
11. If my son (was, were) more ambitious, he would at least take the practice test once.
12. We requested that we (are, be) given money instead of time off.

Name _____ Date _____

CHAPTER 17 Using Verbs Review

EXERCISE Read the passage and choose the word or group of words that belongs in each underlined space. Write the letter of the correct answer.

(1) Twentieth-century sculpture was more abstract than realistic, especially when artists _____ the human form. (2) Henry Moore, for example, _____ huge reclining figures from wood and stone. (3) Alberto Giacometti _____ for his bronzes of painfully thin, elongated figures. (4) In addition, artists such as Richard Stankiewicz _____ human shapes from boilers, wheels, and chains. (5) If it _____ not for the Industrial Revolution, modern sculptures of people might still resemble those of the Renaissance.

_____ 1. A had depicted
B are depicting
C depicted
D depict

_____ 2. A had been fashioning
B fashioned
C will fashion
D do fashion

_____ 3. A was known
B are known
C was knowed
D be known

_____ 4. A constructed
B are constructing
C construct
D had constructed

_____ 5. A was
B be
C is
D were

By 1619, all free colonists (6) _____ land of their own, and as a result Jamestown (7) _____. In that same year, the leaders (8) _____ the House of Burgesses to make laws and plan for the future. Together with Governor George Yeardley and his council, this combined lawmaking body (9) _____ the General Assembly of Virginia. It (10) _____ the first representative legislature in America.

_____ 6. A granted
B was granted
C had been granted

_____ 7. A flourishes
B flourished
C had flourished

_____ 8. A have been formed
B have formed
C formed

_____ 9. A become
B has become
C became

_____ 10. A is
B was
C has been

Name _____   Date _____

CHAPTER 18   The Nominative Case of Pronouns

[18A] **Case** is the form of a noun or a pronoun that indicates its use in a sentence.
[18A.1] The **nominative case** is used for subjects and predicate nominatives.

> **EXERCISE** Underline the nominative pronoun in each sentence. Then choose the answer that indicates how it is being used in the following sentences.

_____ 1. Were they the women in the movie?
    A subject   B predicate nominative   C appositive

_____ 2. We swimmers were happy to get into the hot showers.
    A subject   B predicate nominative   C appositive

_____ 3. Two junior divers, Tina and I, will be at the swimming meet.
    A subject   B predicate nominative   C appositive

_____ 4. The only people on time this morning were Dick and I.
    A subject   B predicate nominative   C appositive

_____ 5. Neither Miguel nor I saw the plane through the cloud layer.
    A subject   B predicate nominative   C appositive

_____ 6. The first people on board the tour bus were Sam and he.
    A subject   B predicate nominative   C appositive

_____ 7. Both Bret and she sat on the sidelines during the football game.
    A subject   B predicate nominative   C appositive

_____ 8. Mr. Parkinson told Aunt Mary that he had won the lottery.
    A subject   B predicate nominative   C appositive

_____ 9. The gymnasts, Bev, Nancy, and she, all practiced in the gym today.
    A subject   B predicate nominative   C appositive

_____ 10. The only joggers in this group are Jon and I.
    A subject   B predicate nominative   C appositive

_____ 11. Are she and Chris going to the movies with Jack?
    A subject   B predicate nominative   C appositive

_____ 12. Two members of the chorus, Ben and she, will sing a duet.
    A subject   B predicate nominative   C appositive

_____ 13. Because the alarm clock stopped, they missed their ride.
    A subject   B predicate nominative   C appositive

CHAPTER 18 The Nominative Case of Pronouns

EXERCISE A Choose the correct form of the pronoun in parentheses.

_____ 1. Rita and (I, me) prefer detective stories to science fiction.

_____ 2. That is (he, him) in the green blazer and the white shoes.

_____ 3. Two team members, Fred and (him, he), are featured in this morning's newspaper.

_____ 4. Are you positive it was (her, she) in the back of the boat?

_____ 5. Did Diana and (she, her) send you a postcard from Denver?

_____ 6. Lee and (me, I) took our driving tests at the same time.

_____ 7. (He, Him) and I are the only two without season seats.

_____ 8. (We, Us) three together can certainly lift that big box.

_____ 9. Neither Clarence nor (I, me) has a ride to the prom this weekend.

_____ 10. Without your help (us, we) hikers would not have found the trail.

_____ 11. The people at the top of the stairs must have been (they, them).

_____ 12. Wally and (him, he) will show you the best ski trails.

_____ 13. Both Sarah and (she, her) are running for the same office.

_____ 14. Have you and (him, he) met everyone here this evening?

_____ 15. The students chosen for the solos were Josh and (she, her).

EXERCISE B Rewrite the following sentences, correcting any errors in the use of pronouns. If a sentence is correct, write C.

16. Is that her with all the books?

17. Two friends, Pam and her, quizzed me for an hour.

18. Did the teacher tell you that we students need pencils?

19. I'm sure it was him who finished before the rest of us.

20. The youngest students at the exam were Gina and me.

Name _____ Date _____

CHAPTER 18 — The Objective Case of Pronouns

[18A.4] The **objective case** is used for direct objects, indirect objects, objects of prepositions, and objects of verbals.

> **EXERCISE** Decide how the following pronouns are being used in the sentence and write DO (direct object), IO (indirect object), OP (object of the preposition), or OV (object of a verbal) in the blank. Then circle the objective case of the pronoun.

_____ 1. Did Mr. Ford lend Vic or (he, him) the key to the room?

_____ 2. Mr. Goza gave Blanche and (I, me) our costumes for the class play.

_____ 3. Can you find Ruth and (I, me) in this picture?

_____ 4. Elise demonstrated origami to Joan and (us, we).

_____ 5. Between Kim and (she, her), you don't have a chance.

_____ 6. Greg brought Steve and (she, her) some oranges from Florida.

_____ 7. Hailing (me, I) from the porch, Carlos pointed to an empty seat.

_____ 8. The clear sky looked good to Charlene and (me, I).

_____ 9. The Brenners warmly congratulated Wendy and (we, us).

_____ 10. Mr. Hall's goat chased Gabe and (I, me) across the pasture.

_____ 11. Billy peeked at Chris and (I, me) from the kitchen.

_____ 12. The signs at the pond warned Mary and (she, her).

_____ 13. Mr. Kohn gave April and (he, him) his old computer.

_____ 14. Other students are sure to help (me, I) decorate the room.

_____ 15. Frank offered Christine and (he, him) a lift to the pool.

_____ 16. Ms. Edgerly gave Lu Ann and (we, us) this advice: "Have fun."

_____ 17. The skates belong to (us, we).

_____ 18. Are you going swimming with Bruce and (I, me)?

_____ 19. According to (he, him) that show is on television tonight.

_____ 20. Don't start home without (she, her).

Name _____ Date _____

CHAPTER 18 The Objective Case of Pronouns

EXERCISE A Cross out any incorrect pronouns in the following sentences and write the correct pronoun in the blank. If a sentence is correct, write C.

_____ 1. Why don't you ask three people—Mary, Ron, and he—to watch for the car?

_____ 2. The car headlights will warn we guests.

_____ 3. Seeing they drive up, we ducked behind the furniture.

_____ 4. Ron gave Wendy and I the special signal.

_____ 5. Do you have any story ideas for Joe or I?

_____ 6. By carrying them over the Alps, Hannibal's elephants enabled his soldiers to attack Rome.

_____ 7. Scientists use radio telescopes to bring they data from other galaxies.

_____ 8. Seeing them fishing from the bridge, Ms. Faurot joined in.

_____ 9. Would you take a picture of Katie and I?

EXERCISE B Read the following passage. Cross out any incorrect pronouns and write the correct case above.

Last week my dad took my sister Maya and I to see the Statue of Liberty in New York City. First, we boarded a ferry from Battery Park to Liberty Island. My dad and me really liked the boat ride, but Maya didn't like the rocking motion of the boat. Maya was amazed by how big the statue really was! I took a picture of she and my dad in the promenade on Ft. Wood, the building underneath the statue. Then a park ranger gave we a tour of the museum inside the pedestal of the statue. Dad and I enjoyed seeing the original 1886 torch. Dad told Maya and I the story of how he visited the statue with his parents who immigrated to America from Costa Rica. We all climbed the stairs to the crown. What an amazing view! My dad could not speak but just smiled at my sister and I. Us Americans can be proud of our beautiful Lady Liberty.

Name _____ Date _____

CHAPTER 18 — The Possessive Case of Pronouns

[18A.8] The **possessive case** is used to show ownership or possession.

EXERCISE A Circle the correct word in parentheses.

1. (Your, You're) gloves are on the hall table.
2. What did you think of (his, him) winning a gold medal?
3. What time does (you're, your) watch say now?
4. No one was surprised at (me, my) arriving an hour late.
5. All the guests hung (their, they're) coats on the rack by the front door.
6. The lunch in that picnic basket must be (theirs, there's).
7. Did you read about (my, me) swimming in the channel?
8. I heard about (them, their) giving a ride to the twins.
9. The raccoon had (it's, its) head in the garbage can.
10. (Theirs, There's) is our school's only entry in the race.

EXERCISE B Complete the following sentences with an appropriate posssesive case pronoun. Answers will vary.

11. After the party, _____ were the only balloons with air in them.
12. All the snakes at the zoo have shed _____ skins.
13. I am all for _____ driving here for the weekend.
14. Did you hear about _____ catching a twelve-inch pike?
15. That photograph on the bulletin board is one of _____.
16. We were delighted to learn of _____ getting the door prize.
17. The turkeys all have _____ wings clipped.
18. Did you sign _____ name to the petition?
19. Were you surprised at _____ playing the piano at the party?
20. _____ parents drove to Florida and back in one week.

Name _____   Date _____

CHAPTER 18 — Nominative, Objective, and Possessive Case Pronouns

EXERCISE Complete each sentence by circling the correct pronoun.

1. The automatic burglar alarm will warn (we, us) owners.

2. We latecomers are finding (them, our) seats in the dark.

3. (She, Her) buying her ticket early saved half an hour.

4. Two true champions, Arthur and (she, her), stood smiling on the stage.

5. Conor and he were invited to join (them, their) row.

6. The silence after the movie proved (it's, its) impact upon the audience.

7. This soda is mine, but where is (your's, yours)?

8. There's little likelihood of (their, us) seeing this movie in our small hometown.

9. Are (she and I, her and me) going to go Brown University in the fall?

10. We friends try to save (us, our) shared time off from work for movie dates.

Name _____ Date _____

CHAPTER 18 *Who* and *Whom* in Clauses

[18B.1] The correct case of *who* is determined by how the pronoun is used in a question or a clause.

EXERCISE A Decide how *who* or *whom* is used in the sentence by writing S (subject), DO (direct object), or OP (object of the preposition). Then underline the correct form of the pronoun in parentheses.

_____ 1. From (who, whom) did you learn my name?

_____ 2. For (who, whom) will you vote in the next election?

_____ 3. (Who, Whom) did you see at the basketball game yesterday?

_____ 4. To (who, whom) did you send your application?

_____ 5. After work, (who, whom) will you take to the skating rink?

_____ 6. (Who, Whom) did you think arrived first?

_____ 7. (Who, Whom) did you notify?

_____ 8. With (who, whom) do you plan to drive to Madison?

_____ 9. (Who, Whom) did you choose as your fencing partner?

_____ 10. After the snowstorm is over, (who, whom) will clear the sidewalk?

_____ 11. At the banquet, (who, whom) did you introduce first?

_____ 12. With (who, whom) did you practice squash today?

_____ 13. (Who, Whom) do you suppose will be elected governor?

_____ 14. (Who, Whom) in your opinion is the best pitcher in the league?

_____ 15. (Who, Whom) did they take to the concert last night?

EXERCISE B Write five sentences that follow the directions below.

1. Begin a question with *who*.

_____

2. Begin a question with *whom* used as a direct object.

_____

3. Include *who* as the subject of a subordinate clause.

_____

4. Use *whom* as the direct object in a subordinate clause.

_____

5. Include *whom* as an object of a preposition in a subordinate clause.

_____

Name _____ Date _____

CHAPTER 18 Pronouns in Elliptical Clauses

[18B.2] An **elliptical clause** is a subordinate clause that begins with *than* or *as* and has words omitted. The omitted words are understood to be there.

EXERCISE A Underline the pronoun that correctly completes the elliptical clause.

1. You can certainly run faster than (I, me).

2. No one likes Swiss cheese more than (I, me).

3. No runner is as fast as (him, he).

4. Do you think Nita is as good a bowler as (her, she)?

5. After the game Rose was calmer than (I, me).

6. Now that the test is over, are you as happy as (we, us)?

7. Don won because he is a better player than (me, I).

8. Peggy believes Emily is taller than (her, she).

9. I think we will be later than (they, them).

10. They certainly sail better than (we, us).

11. No one has redder hair than (him, he).

12. All the judges gave him more points than (I, me).

13. No one reads as fast as (her, she).

14. Do you think Vic is a better piano player than (me, I)?

15. Diandra received a better grade than (me, I).

EXERCISE B Complete each sentence using the pronoun that correctly completes the elliptical clause.

16. Did you sell as many subscriptions as _____?

17. Sandy studied French as long as _____.

18. Are you sure Max is stronger than _____?

19. Have you spent as much time at the computer keyboard as _____?

20. Dolly spent as much time worrying as _____.

Name _____ Date _____

CHAPTER 18 Pronouns and Their Antecedents

[18C.1] A single pronoun must agree in **number** and **gender** with its antecedent.

> **EXERCISE A** Circle the pronoun in parentheses that correctly agrees in number and gender with its antecedent.

1. Neither Mark nor the Davis brothers have (his, their) licenses.

2. Both Donna and Elisabeth have (her, their) uniforms on.

3. Will either Rob or Jack play (his, their) guitar this evening?

4. Neither Edith nor her sisters have (her, their) sunglasses on.

5. Will Jan or Carla mail (her, their) résumé to the company?

6. Every painting in the gallery had (its, their) own light over it.

7. Either his sisters or Andy will loan you (his, their) car.

8. Both Juan and Jerry will do (his, their) best to help you.

9. Neither Paul nor Chung wants to loan (his, their) equipment.

10. Either Ruth or Audrey left (her, their) lunch in the car.

> **EXERCISE B** Complete the following sentences with an appropriate pronoun.

11. The Great Wallendas performed _____ aerial acts skillfully.

12. Karl Wallenda learned _____ profession in Germany.

13. His wife Helen owed _____ success to both courage and skill.

14. Karl and Helen left _____ native Germany to perform in the United States.

15. Other members of the family dedicated _____ lives to performing on the high wire.

16. Many troupes used a safety net, but the Wallendas performed without _____.

17. In one act both Joe and Herman Wallenda rode _____ bicycles on the high wire.

18. The two bicyclists supported Karl on a pole between _____.

CHAPTER 18 Indefinite Pronouns as Antecedents

EXERCISE Underline the pronoun that correctly completes each sentence.

1. Some of the uniforms had numbers on _____. (it, **them**)

2. Everybody in the boys' chorus had _____ music. (their, **his**)

3. Few of the girls on the team had taken _____ seats on the bus. (**their**, her)

4. None of the bottles of soda have lost _____ fizz. (its, **their**)

5. At the service station, he asked one of the men to put air in _____ tires. (**his**, their)

6. Several of my teachers performed _____ songs on stage. (its, **their**)

7. Somebody on the girls' debating team has lost _____ voice. (their, **her**)

8. Each of the boys took _____ turn at bat. (their, **his**)

9. Few of the kittens have had _____ shots as yet. (**their**, its)

10. Both of the women wrote _____ own campaign speeches. (**their**, her)

11. Some of the apples have spots on _____ skins. (its, **their**)

12. Most of the milk has lost _____ freshness. (their, **its**)

13. All of the blueberry bushes have dropped _____ berries. (its, **their**)

14. Somebody on the boys' gymnastic team lost _____ balance. (**his**, their)

15. Both of these cars need _____ oil changed soon. (its, **their**)

CHAPTER 18 — Unclear, Missing, or Confusing Antecedents

EXERCISE Decide if the following sentences contain unclear, missing, or confusing antecedents. Write C on the line if the sentence is correct. If the sentence is incorrect, rewrite it correctly on the line.

1. I ate a strawberry and a peach and enjoyed it.

2. In Florida they have many birds.

3. I speak with an English accent because I am from there.

4. I wore a jacket to the game because it was windy.

5. Tony looked through the catalog and decided on those he wanted to order.

6. We went to the beach on Saturday, and it was beautiful.

7. In the instruction manual, it shows how to fix the faucet.

8. The bands played jazz and blues music; I like them both.

9. They have many records in that store.

10. I like planting a vegetable garden because you get to eat what you grow.

11. My favorite food is asparagus, but neither of my brothers likes it.

12. We enjoyed the nighttime sky above the lake, and we spent hours staring at it.

Name _____ Date _____

CHAPTER 18 — Using Pronouns Review

EXERCISE A Underline the pronoun in parentheses that correctly completes each sentence.

1. Both Apollo and Artemis drove (her, **their**) chariots.

2. The sun chose (**its**, it's) path behind Apollo.

3. Apollo played (**his**, their) lyre for entertainment.

4. All who participated in the Olympic Games competed at (his, **their**) best to honor the gods.

5. I see that (you, **your**) running has benefits.

6. (**We**, Us) marathoners feel thrilled to finish.

7. One of the girls practices at (**her**, their) school.

8. Give (**whoever**, whomever) asks more water.

9. (**Who**, Whom) do you think will win the race?

10. The runner (**who**, whom) is favored to win is (**he**, him).

11. (Me and him, **He and I**) will stand at the finish line and help the runners.

12. Give the ribbons to (**whoever**, whomever) finishes the race.

13. The food over there is for (we, **us**) volunteers.

14. The volunteers for the race are (her, **she**) and (**I**, me).

EXERCISE B Read the passage and circle the correct pronoun.

On the night of the awards ceremony, the students marched in and took **(15)** (their, **his or her**) seats. When Mrs. Graham reached for the first award and there were none, no one was more surprised than **(16)** (her, **she**). Seeing **(17)** (**them**, they) nowhere on the stage, Mrs. Graham began handing out imaginary awards. First **(18)** (**she**, her) called Jason's name and handed **(19)** (himself, **him**) his imaginary award. "I want to thank everyone," **(20)** (**he**, him) said, "for this imaginary award."

Name _____ Date _____

CHAPTER 19 Agreement of Subjects and Verbs

[19A] A verb must agree with its subject in number.

EXERCISE A Circle the subject and underline the correct form of the verb.

1. Wood (was, were) human beings' first fuel.

2. They (was, were) burning wood thousands of years ago.

3. These early hunters (was, were) also using wood fires to cook meat.

4. Some people still (heats, heat) their homes with wood.

5. As long as 2,000 years ago, coal (was, were) used as fuel.

6. It (was, were) also burned to make steam for steam engines.

7. Today burning coal (produces, produce) steam to generate electricity.

8. Many people (uses, use) charcoal in outdoor grills.

9. Most liquid fuels (comes, come) from oil.

10. Spacecrafts (is, are) fueled by a mixture of liquid oxygen and kerosene.

EXERCISE B In the following paragraph, underline the correct verb in parentheses.

Americans (has, have) fresh fruit available all year long. In the United States, the most popular fruits (is, are) apples, oranges, and bananas. Apples (is, are) grown in many northern states. Oranges (come, comes) from warmer areas. Bananas (is, are) imported from Central and South America. Some fruit (is, are) made into jelly and jam. Stone fruits (is, are) some of the most popular ones to use in sandwich and toast spreads.

Name _____ Date _____

CHAPTER 19 Agreement and Interrupting Words

[19A.4] The agreement of a verb and subject is not changed by any interrupting words.

EXERCISE A Underline the subject. Circle the correct verb.

1. The frog, like other amphibious creatures, (lives, live) both in water and on land.

2. The tadpoles swimming around any ordinary pond (is, are) our future frogs.

3. Frogs living on the bark of a tree (has, have) a similar coloring to the bark.

4. Some frogs, like the giant African frog, (weighs, weigh) up to ten pounds.

5. The largest of all American frogs (is, are) the bullfrog.

6. A bullfrog in one of Mark Twain's stories (was, were) filled with lead shot.

7. The otherwise excellent jumper, when weighted down with all those pellets, (was, were) not able to jump an inch.

8. Bullfrogs in top form (jumps, jump) twenty times the length of their bodies.

9. Frogs, inhabiting all areas of the world, (is, are) hardy creatures.

10. A frog, like human beings, (breathes, breath) through lungs.

EXERCISE B In the following paragraph, underline the subject in each sentence and circle the correct verb.

All reptiles, such as the frog, (has, have) to hibernate. These cold-blooded creatures, hibernating in underwater mud, (absorbs, absorb) oxygen through their skin. Animals in a state of hibernation (needs, need) no food. The frog in several ways (is, are) different from the toad. The frog, unlike its toad cousins, (has, have) a smooth, moist skin. Toads in America (has, have) dry, rough skin.

Name _____ Date _____

CHAPTER 19 — Compound Subjects

[19B.1] When subjects are joined by *or, nor, either/or,* or *neither/nor*, the verb agrees with the closer subject.

[19B.2] When subjects are joined by *and* or *both/and*, the verb is plural.

EXERCISE Choose the correct form of the verb in parentheses.

1. Forsythia and crocuses (is, are) early signs of spring.

2. Bagels and lox (is, are) a favorite meal for breakfast.

3. Every man, woman, and child (was, were) rescued.

4. Either Ron or his parents (is, are) going to pay.

5. Neither our team nor their team (has, have) scored so far.

6. Either my father or she (is, are) going to the conference.

7. My counselor and math teacher (is, are) married to each other.

8. One skinned knee and two scratched legs (was, were) our total casualties.

9. Both prefixes and suffixes (is, are) part of many words.

10. Terry and her friends (is, are) coming over this afternoon.

11. Swallows and bats (is, are) eating flies high over our lawn.

12. Both fine balance and timing (is, are) required in pole vaulting.

13. Neither President Washington nor President Truman (was, were) a college graduate.

14. Each peach and plum in this bowl (is, are) ripe.

15. Either our three wells or our reservoir (is, are) sufficient.

CHAPTER 19 Compound Subjects

EXERCISE Decide if the verb in each of the following sentences agrees with its subjects. If the verb is correct, write C (correct) in the blank. If it is incorrect, write the correct verb form in the blank.

_____ 1. The three oaks and the Japanese maple has red leaves.

_____ 2. Each knife and fork were carefully placed on the place mats.

_____ 3. A sweatband and leather shoes are the mark of a true jogger.

_____ 4. Are Jack and the twins going to watch the tournament?

_____ 5. Neither Lewis nor his parents is going to the open house.

_____ 6. My companions and my best friend are out of town.

_____ 7. Waffles and sausage are Betty's favorite breakfast.

_____ 8. At sunup the grass and the cobwebs were glistening with dew.

_____ 9. Both Jamie and Dixie are going to visit the campus today.

_____ 10. Each apple and peach is picked by hand.

_____ 11. Neither the coconut nor the avocado is grown here.

_____ 12. Either our guide or two philosophers is showing up tomorrow.

_____ 13. Every high jumper and pole-vaulter is required to report for a physical.

_____ 14. Is either Chip or the triplets going to enter the three-legged race?

_____ 15. Every sailor and passenger are required to report for lifeboat practice.

CHAPTER 19 Indefinite Pronouns as Subjects

[19B.3] A verb must agree in number with an indefinite pronoun used as a subject.

EXERCISE A Label the underlined subjects in the following sentences as *singular* (S), *plural* (P), or *either* (E). If the subject can be either singular or plural, circle the word used to determine the correct verb. Finally, circle the correct verb in parentheses.

_____ 1. Anyone (is, are) eligible for the computer course.

_____ 2. Everyone (comes, come) to the aquarium eventually.

_____ 3. Many of my friends (has, have) moved away.

_____ 4. Everybody (has, have) to pass the swimming test to graduate.

_____ 5. Somebody (is, are) responsible for noting the temperature.

_____ 6. Most of the cars in this lot (is, are) late models.

_____ 7. Some of Browning's poems (was, were) written when he was over eighty.

_____ 8. Most of us (goes, go) out for track.

_____ 9. A few of the baseball gloves (looks, look) new.

_____ 10. Several of the weather satellites (is, are) working perfectly.

EXERCISE B In the following paragraph, cross out five incorrect verbs and write the correct verbs above.

The picnic was a disaster. When the picnic committee were discussing who would bring what kind of food, they argued for an hour. Finally, they chose three people to be the food committee. This small group were able to decide on the menu in five minutes. Then came the day of the picnic—bright and sunny. None of the hamburgers was made ahead of time. Several of the cookies was lost to ants before anyone noticed. Most of the ice was melting because it was left in the sun. Somebody in the park were setting off fireworks. Both of the picnic tables were coated in wet, dirty leaves and ants.

Name _____   Date _____

CHAPTER 19 — Subjects in Inverted Order

[19B.4] The subject and the verb of an inverted sentence must agree in number.

EXERCISE A Choose the letter that represents the subject of the sentence.

_____ 1. On the Egyptian woman's head was a tall water jug.
  A woman
  B head
  C jug

_____ 2. How do Barbara and Henry like the new gym?
  A Barbara
  B Barbara, Henry
  C gym

_____ 3. Entirely within the border of the United States there is just one of the Great Lakes—Lake Michigan.
  A border
  B one
  C Lake Michigan

_____ 4. Were you ever in a desert after a rain?
  A Were
  B you
  C desert

_____ 5. Across many rivers in New England are covered bridges.
  A rivers
  B New England
  C bridges

EXERCISE B In the following paragraph, underline the correct form of each verb.

When (is, are) most English-speaking readers ever going to experience bullfighting as the author Ernest Hemingway did? In each book (is, are) the spirit of the famous American author. There (is, are) many writers of the Lost Generation besides Hemingway, but only he was able to capture the sport of bullfighting. In *Death in the Afternoon* (is, are) vivid images of bullfighting. (Was, Were) you ever able to read his novel *The Sun Also Rises*? In this book, as well, (is, are) many sports themes. Realistic dialogue (is, are) a notable feature of his books. There (is, are) many European settings used by Hemingway that make it of special interest. Some of these (is, are) France, Spain, and Italy. (Do, Does) you have an interest in other aspects of Spain besides bullfighting? If so, when (is, are) you going to make time to read his book *For Whom the Bell Tolls*?

Name _____ Date _____

CHAPTER 19 Other Agreement Problems

[19C.1] Use a singular verb with a collective noun subject that is thought of as a unit. Use a plural verb with a collective noun subject that is thought of as individual parts.
[19C.2] A subject that expresses an amount, a measurement, a weight, or a time is usually considered singular and takes a singular verb.
[19C.3] Use a singular verb with *the number of* and a plural verb with *a number of*.

> **EXERCISE** Circle the subject and underline the verb that agrees with the underlined collective noun subject.

1. One hundred kilometers per hour (is, are) approximately equal to sixty miles per hour.

2. The congregation (is, are) gathering for a parade.

3. The number of Olympic gold medals won by Chinese athletes (is, are) increasing.

4. Our bobsled team (is, are) determined to win.

5. The number of Third World countries in the United Nations (has, have) greatly increased.

6. A number of climbers (has, have) reached the summit.

7. The orchestra (is, are) playing the school song.

8. Our football team (has, have) come from behind.

9. In the United States, the number of citizens voting (is, are) shamefully small.

10. Only two-thirds of the orchestra (is, are) here.

11. Our tennis team (has, have) gone to their rooms for a siesta.

12. The jury (has, have) reached a verdict.

13. The first couple on the dance floor (was, were) Nadine and Gerry.

14. The band (is, are) tuning their instruments.

15. The basketball team (is, are) having a hard time finding the hoops tonight.

16. A number of acorns (has, have) been stored away by that squirrel.

17. Thirty pounds (is, are) a heavy weight to carry in a knapsack.

Name _____ Date _____

CHAPTER 19 — Other Agreement Problems

[19C.4] Use a singular verb with certain subjects that are plural in form but singular in meaning.
[19C.5] The verb part of a contraction must agree in number with the subject.
[19C.6] A verb agrees with the subject of a sentence, not with the predicate nominative.
[19C.7] A title is singular and takes a singular verb.

EXERCISE Circle the correct answer.

1. Civics (is, are) a social science dealing with the rights and duties of citizens.

2. *Strange Stories, Amazing Facts* (contains, contain) some astonishing information.

3. (Doesn't, Don't) Guatemala raise most of the chicle used in chewing gum?

4. The mayor (doesn't, don't) agree with that proposition.

5. Komodo dragons (is, are) actually monitor lizards.

6. Two chemists, Lea and Perrins, (was, were) the creators of Worcestershire sauce.

7. Gymnastics (is, are) a sport in which Romanians excel.

8. *Three Kingdoms* (traces, trace) the decline of the Han Dynasty in China.

9. The elephants (is, are) a favorite attraction at the zoo.

10. The United States (is, are) a nation of immigrants.

11. He (doesn't, don't) have permission to swim in this reservoir.

12. Eighty years ago mules and horses (was, were) the power that pulled the plow.

13. Books (is, are) a great pleasure for interested readers.

14. Social studies (is, are) a field that its experts call a science.

15. Mary says her house is haunted, but Jonas and Keisha (doesn't, don't) believe her.

16. *The Old Revolutionaries* (tells, tell) about some leaders of the American Revolution.

17. Sauces (is, are) a pleasure to create.

18. (Doesn't, Don't) the raspberries on top of that cake look tasty?

CHAPTER 19 Subject and Verb Agreement Review

EXERCISE A Write C if the subject and verb agreement is correct and I if it is incorrect. Write the correct version of the verb on the line.

_____ 1. Neither Raymond nor the Martinez brothers are running in the election.

_____ 2. Here are the tomatoes from our garden.

_____ 3. Each student in my class are finally finished.

_____ 4. Politics is the downfall of many friendships.

_____ 5. Both the corn and the beans receives water from our irrigation system.

_____ 6. A number of people still reads poetry every day.

_____ 7. Eighty miles per hour seem awfully fast to an armchair traveler like me.

_____ 8. Straddling many small rivers and streams in southern Iowa is covered bridges.

_____ 9. None of the hamburgers have been cooked yet.

_____ 10. *Wuthering Heights* by Emily Brontë are a wonderful gothic romance.

EXERCISE B Underline the verbs that do not agree with the subjects. Then write those verbs correctly.

Authors such as J.R.R. Tolkien and C.S. Lewis has created unforgettable fantasy lands. *The Hobbit* is filled with places such as the Lonely Mountain, the Iron Hills, and Wilderland. In *The Lion, the Witch, and the Wardrobe*, Peter, Susan, Edmund, and Lucy discovers a fascinating world called Narnia. When you looks at your surroundings through the eyes of a writer like Tolkien, the world of dreams envelopes you. How does young readers ever return to the real world after experiencing such a feast of the imagination?

Name _____ Date _____

CHAPTER 20 • Regular Comparisons

[20A.1] Add **-er** to form the comparative degree and **-est** to form the superlative degree of one-syllable modifiers.

[20A.2] Use **-er** or **more** to form the comparative and **-est** or **most** to form the superlative degree of two-syllable modifiers.

[20A.3] Use **more** to form the comparative and **most** to form the superlative degree of modifiers with three or more syllables.

EXERCISE A Write the comparative form of each of the following words.

1. helpful _____
2. loud _____
3. easy _____
4. steady _____
5. deep _____
6. messy _____
7. noisily _____
8. usual _____
9. contented _____
10. comfortable _____

EXERCISE B Write the superlative form of each of the following words.

11. nice _____
12. rare _____
13. fanciful _____
14. crazy _____
15. woolly _____
16. commonly _____
17. colorful _____
18. dark _____
19. violent _____
20. fashionable _____

Name _____ Date _____

CHAPTER 20 Regular Comparisons

EXERCISE A Circle the correct form of the modifier in parentheses.

1. Antarctica is the (less, least) fertile of all the continents.
2. Herman must be the (more, most) awkward skater in the world.
3. Shrews are (less, least) peaceful than manatees.
4. Jacob thought his trip was (more, most) interesting than Sasha's.
5. It is (more, most) convenient for me to meet you at the library than at the school.
6. Marta knows (less, least) about basketball than Kim does.
7. Of the four Steve is the (less, least) likely candidate to win the election.
8. The barometric pressure drops (more, most) steadily when it is about to rain than when it is sunny.
9. Our teacher suggested that it would be (more, most) beneficial if we got a good night's sleep before the science midterm, rather than cramming all night.
10. Carlos thought that chocolate-covered ants were the (less, least) appealing candy he could imagine.
11. The (more, most) inspiring book I ever read was *Three Cups of Tea*.
12. My brother's (less, least) favorite sport to watch on television is golf.
13. Some historians believe that Julius Caesar was the (more, most) brilliant military leader of all time.
14. It is (more, most) tragic to have loved and lost than never to have loved at all.
15. Who is (less, least) likely to succeed in the legislature—Tom Morain or Steve Zinn?

EXERCISE B Read the following paragraph. Underline the correct form of the modifier in parentheses.

One type of monitor lizard, also known as the Komodo dragon, is (longer, longest) than any other lizard. It reaches (almost nearly, nearly) ten feet from nose to tail, and (often, oftener) weighs 300 pounds. (Least dangerous, Less dangerous) Komodo dragons can overpower and eat (smaller, smallest) deer, wild pigs, and even water buffalo.

Name _____   Date _____

CHAPTER 20 — Irregular Comparisons

EXERCISE Choose the proper comparison modifier that completes the following sentences.

____ 1. Joel spends _____ hours in the computer lab than anyone else.
   A many
   B more
   C most

____ 2. The engine in his car sounds _____ than last week.
   A bad
   B worse
   C worst

____ 3. That aquarium has the _____ fish I have ever seen in an aquarium of that size.
   A many
   B more
   C most

____ 4. The air over this city contains _____ pollution.
   A little
   B less
   C least

____ 5. That suit really looks _____ on you.
   A good
   B better
   C best

____ 6. Tom does his _____ work when he really concentrates.
   A good
   B better
   C best

____ 7. Shane served _____ after losing the first set.
   A bad
   B badly
   C worse

____ 8. There are _____ blooming trees in the park.
   A many
   B more
   C most

____ 9. Chocolate ice cream is my _____ favorite flavor.
   A little
   B less
   C least

____ 10. Paul's chances of winning the raffle are ___ now that Sammy has bought ten tickets.
   A bad
   B worse
   C worst

____ 11. Paula has broken the _____ track records of any team member.
   A many
   B more
   C most

____ 12. Some people believe that French cooking is the _____ cuisine in the world.
   A good
   B better
   C best

____ 13. In the spring the garden is filled with _____ different types of flowers.
   A many
   B more
   C most

____ 14. Now that I have joined the gymnastics club, I have _____ time to talk on the telephone than I did before.
   A little
   B less
   C least

____ 15. Tyrannosaurus Rex weighed _____ than seven tons.
   A much
   B more
   C most

104   Grade 11 • Chapter 20: Using Adjectives and Adverbs

Name _____ Date _____

CHAPTER 20 Irregular Comparisons

EXERCISE A Circle the comparison modifier that correctly completes each sentence.

1. The prognosis for a quick recovery was (good, better, best) than Morgan had thought.
2. One of the (many, more, most) outstanding medical contributions to humankind was the Salk vaccine.
3. Brandon was a (little, less, least) apprehensive before his concert.
4. Greece is (many, more, most) mountainous than Saudi Arabia.
5. It is (bad, worse, worst) to drive in sleet than in rain.
6. The (many, more, most) popular form of transportation in China is the bicycle.
7. A computer is (many, more, most) complex than the human brain.
8. The sinking of the *Titanic* was one of the (bad, worse, worst) disasters in maritime history.
9. Young chimps spend (many, more, most) of the time chasing each other.
10. You look (bad, worse, worst) in the red shirt than in the beige.
11. Ernesto has (bad, worse, worst) migraine headaches.
12. The (many, more, most) books she reads, the better educated she will be.

EXERCISE B In the following paragraph, choose the correct form of the modifier in parentheses.

At Kitty Hawk, the Wright brothers aimed to prove that planes could **(13)** _____ be flown by skilled pilots. The brothers worked on bicycles before they worked on **(14)** _____ planes. Which did the brothers like **(15)** _____, building bicycles or building airplanes? Airplanes, of course! A 62-minute flight in 1908 made Orville an international celebrity, perhaps **(16)** _____ than he expected. The brothers achieved greater success **(17)** _____ than aviation experts. Orville Wright lived 36 years **(18)** _____ than his brother Wilbur.

_____ 13. **A** most best   **B** bestest   **C** better   **D** best

_____ 14. **A** most   **B** many   **C** much   **D** more

_____ 15. **A** least   **B** worst   **C** better   **D** less

_____ 16. **A** more sooner   **B** sooner   **C** less soon   **D** better

_____ 17. **A** quickly   **B** more quickly   **C** quicker   **D** quickest

_____ 18. **A** longest   **B** more longer   **C** long   **D** longer

CHAPTER 20 Problems with Comparisons

[20B.1] Do not use both *-er* and *more* to form the comparative degree, or both *-est* and *most* to form the superlative degree of modifiers.

[20B.3] Add *other* or *else* when comparing a member of a group with the rest of the group.

EXERCISE A Underline the form of the modifier in parentheses that completes each sentence correctly.

1. The emerald is the (softest, more softest) of all precious stones.
2. North Carolina is (bigger, more bigger) than South Carolina.
3. Is an owl actually wiser than (any, any other) bird?
4. Your float is the (grandest, most grandest) one in the parade.
5. The life span of a sea turtle is (greater, more greater) than that of a shark.
6. This neighborhood is quieter than (any, any other) in the city.
7. Paul can play the trumpet better than (anyone, anyone else) in the band.
8. Greek history goes (further, more further) back than Roman history.
9. The Metropolitan Museum of Art contains many of the (finest, most finest) paintings in the world.
10. This chipmunk is the (boldest, most boldest) one in the yard.
11. Tina cheers louder than (anyone, anyone else) in the bleachers.
12. Round Pond is (safer, more safer) for skating than Mystic Lake.
13. Some of the (oldest, most oldest) houses in America are in New England.
14. Is birch bark whiter than (any, any other) bark?
15. The ostrich is larger than (any, any other) bird in the world.

EXERCISE B Underline the correct form of the modifier in parentheses in the following paragraph.

In winter the temperatures are usually higher in Florida than in (any, any other) state. More than (anything, anything else), its balmy winter climate attracts people to the state. Enthusiastic Florida "snowbirds" believe the air is (more clearer, clearer), the days (more longer, longer), and the tropical waters (more cleanest, cleaner) than (anywhere else, anywhere) in the country, except Hawaii. There are many interesting places to visit as well. For example, St. Augustine is one of the (oldest, most oldest) cities in the United States. It is probably visited more than (any, any other) historic site in Florida even though it isn't the (showiest, most showiest).

CHAPTER 20 Problems with Comparisons

[20B.2] Compare only items of a similar kind.

> **EXERCISE** Choose the sentence that correctly uses a comparative modifier.

____ 1. **A** Squirrels' nests look much like eagles.
      B Squirrels' nests look much like eagles' nests.

____ 2. **A** The octopus's beak is as sharp as a parrot.
      B The octopus's beak is as sharp as a parrot's beak.

____ 3. **A** The distance from the equator to the North Pole is the same as the distance from the equator to the South Pole.
      B The distance from the equator to the North Pole is the same as the South Pole.

____ 4. **A** The area of Lake Superior is greater than Lake Huron.
      B The area of Lake Superior is greater than the area of Lake Huron.

____ 5. **A** Idaho's annual potato crop is usually larger than Maine's annual potato crop.
      B Idaho's annual potato crop is usually larger than Maine.

____ 6. **A** The average height of a redwood is greater than an oak.
      B The average height of a redwood is greater than that of an oak.

____ 7. **A** The length of the Danube River is greater than that of the Seine River.
      B The length of the Danube River is greater than the Seine River.

____ 8. **A** The time Earth takes to orbit the sun is longer than Mercury.
      B The time Earth takes to orbit the sun is longer than the time Mercury takes to orbit the sun.

____ 9. **A** Escaping the swift destruction of a forest fire may be easier than escaping the devastation of an earthquake.
      B Escaping the swift destruction of a forest fire may be easier than an earthquake.

____ 10. **A** Fooling the plants into flowering earlier may be more difficult than the beginning gardener.
      B Fooling the plants into flowering earlier may be more difficult than the beginning gardener realizes.

Name _____ Date _____

CHAPTER 20 Problems with Modifiers

[20C] Be aware of special problems when using adjectives and adverbs. It's important to know whether to use an adjective or adverb, *good* or *well*, or *bad* or *badly*. Be alert for double negatives.

EXERCISE A Decide if the following sentences need an adjective (ADJ) or adverb (ADV) modifier and write the correct abbreviation in the blank. Then underline the correct form of the modifier in parentheses.

_____ 1. This parrot can whistle (realistic, realistically) enough to fool my dog.

_____ 2. Larry certainly looks (good, well) in his uniform.

_____ 3. Our grandfather clock has been running (good, well) since it was cleaned.

_____ 4. The golfer aimed very (careful, carefully).

_____ 5. Robby looked (peaceful, peacefully) while he was sleeping.

_____ 6. Those roses smell particularly (good, well).

_____ 7. My partner and I didn't play too (bad, badly) in the volleyball tournament.

_____ 8. I couldn't hear (good, well) from the back row.

_____ 9. Sandy won the relay race (easy, easily).

_____ 10. This watch runs (good, well) under water.

EXERCISE B If the following sentences are correct, write C on the line. If a sentence is incorrect, cross out the modifier and write the correct form on the line.

_____ 11. Franco did very good on his math test.

_____ 12. The farmer shook his fist angrily at the darkening sky.

_____ 13. How good do you know the witness?

_____ 14. Auguste Rodin was a good sculptor.

_____ 15. The baby woke up cheerful from his nap.

_____ 16. My mom told me to drive safe.

_____ 17. Marissa felt well after taking antibiotics for three days.

_____ 18. I found a real nice car for sale on craigslist.

Name _____ Date _____

CHAPTER 20 Double Negatives

[20C.3] Avoid using a double negative.

> **EXERCISE** Write C if a sentence is correct. If it is incorrect, write the sentence correctly on the line.

1. After the snowstorm, there wasn't no one walking on the streets.
   _____

2. That cactus didn't have no blossoms this year.
   _____

3. Walt didn't put nothing on his salad.
   _____

4. I haven't never been so happy in my entire life.
   _____

5. I can barely squeeze under this fence.
   _____

6. On a hazy day, we can't hardly see the mountains from here.
   _____

7. This corn doesn't have no corn silk on it.
   _____

8. Dan can hardly reach the second shelf.
   _____

9. I can scarcely hear the actors from the back row.
   _____

10. Shana hadn't but one mistake on her paper.
    _____

CHAPTER 20 Using Adjectives and Adverbs Review

EXERCISE Write C if the underlined modifiers are correct. If they are not correct, write the correct form on the line.

Those who study oceans have discovered the **(1)** <u>most largest</u> concentrations of old, wrecked ships in the waters around Italy. Some of them go all the way back to **(2)** <u>earlier</u> Rome. Items from one Roman ship included kitchenware, **(3)** <u>finely</u> bronze cups, and two **(4)** <u>more heavy</u> pieces of lead, no doubt parts of a disassembled anchor. The explorers **(5)** <u>had not never</u> anticipated returning to port empty-handed, but their discovery pleased them **(6)** <u>scarcely more</u> than they had expected. In fact, they will probably return to the same area in the future, resuming their search for other ancient, **(7)** <u>wide-traveled</u> vessels.

The use of global positioning systems is a **(8)** <u>most powerfully</u> aid to underwater discovery missions in the twenty-first century. Recent innovations in deep-sea diving technologies make it **(9)** <u>more easier</u> for divers to communicate with the people and machines that track them. In the past, divers actually had to use hand signals to talk with each other, not the **(10)** <u>bestest</u> way to transmit possibly life-and-death information. It's **(11)** <u>more likelier</u> that this technology will be used for things besides exploratory diving, however. The **(12)** <u>least likely</u> use for it will, in fact, be searching through Roman shipwrecks.

1. _____
2. _____
3. _____
4. _____
5. _____
6. _____
7. _____
8. _____
9. _____
10. _____
11. _____
12. _____

CHAPTER 21 Capitalizing Proper Nouns

[21B] Capitalize proper nouns and their abbreviations.

EXERCISE Write the word(s) that should be capitalized in each sentence.

1. Our cat, whiskers, is a calico.

2. It is possible to see the rings of saturn through a telescope.

3. My aunt lives in south carolina.

4. The penobscot river flows through the state of Maine.

5. The howe family has lived in our town for five generations.

6. Last summer we visited many old and famous homes in the city of savannah.

7. The midwest is important to the agricultural industry in this country.

8. The north star is a vital navigational tool for sailors.

9. My family's heritage comes from the country of spain.

10. Every afternoon I take my dog penny to the park to play with other dogs.

11. Every summer my grandfather rents a house on lake summit.

12. Though we live in iowa now, my family's ancestors come from the south.

13. Do you know which is closer to the sun, earth or mars?

14. We drove through the smoky mountains on our way to North Carolina.

15. The Swedish scientists are setting up an outpost at the north pole.

16. We will pass through niagara falls when we travel to Toronto this summer.

17. Our cats harker and mina are actually brother and sister.

CHAPTER 21 Capitalizing Proper Nouns

EXERCISE Choose the word(s) that should be capitalized in each sentence.

_____ 1. The dog lassie starred in several movies made in hollywood.
  A Dog
  B Lassie
  C Lassie, Hollywood

_____ 2. Did larry build a solar home near the city of tucson?
  A Larry
  B Larry, Tucson
  C Larry, City, Tucson

_____ 3. If you go west on river street, you will get to the town of carlyle.
  A West, River, Carlyle
  B River Street, Carlyle
  C River Street, Town, Carlyle

_____ 4. Unlike the moon, earth has oceans such as the atlantic.
  A Moon, Earth, Oceans
  B Moon, Earth, Atlantic
  C Earth, Atlantic

_____ 5. The island of sicily is off the coast of italy.
  A Sicily, Italy
  B Island, Sicily, Italy
  C Island, Sicily, Coast, Italy

_____ 6. We passed through radner township on our way to the pocono mountains.
  A Radner, Pocono
  B Radner, Pocono Mountains
  C Radner Township, Pocono Mountains

_____ 7. The continent of australia is in the pacific ocean.
  A Continent, Australia, Pacific
  B Australia, Pacific Ocean
  C Continent, Australia, Pacific Ocean

_____ 8. The lioness elsa was raised by joy adamson.
  A Joy Adamson
  B Elsa, Joy Adamson
  C Lioness Elsa, Joy Adamson

_____ 9. Do the albyns live in utah?
  A Albyns
  B Albyns, Utah
  C Utah

_____ 10. We visited olympic national park in the state of washington.
  A Olympic, Washington
  B Olympic National Park, State, Washington
  C Olympic National Park, Washington

_____ 11. The island of nantucket lies off the coast of new england.
  A Island, Nantucket, New England
  B Nantucket, New England
  C Island, Nantucket, Coast, New England

_____ 12. The racehorse secretariat won the triple crown in 1973.
  A Secretariat, Triple Crown
  B Racehorse Secretariat, Triple Crown
  C Secretariat

_____ 13. On a clear night, you can see the milky way and the big dipper without a telescope.
  A Milky
  B Milky Way, Big Dipper
  C Milky, Dipper

_____ 14. Many young europeans visit the spanish island of majorca for their summer vacation.
  A Spanish Island, Majorca
  B Europeans, Spanish, Majorca
  C Europeans, Majorca, Summer

CHAPTER 21 Capitalizing Proper Adjectives

[21C] Capitalize most proper adjectives.

EXERCISE Write the word(s) that should be capitalized in each sentence.

1. My spanish class will watch a film on the costa rican rain forest.
2. We just bought a german car with japanese-made tires on it.
3. We ate in a chinese restaurant before attending the performance of the swiss acrobats.
4. The english musicians played elizabethan instruments.
5. Sid has a boston accent, not a midwestern accent.
6. Do you prefer italian dressing or french dressing?
7. The transatlantic flight was completely booked by french tourists.
8. The saturday race will be telecast live on the canadian channel.
9. The pro-british marchers waved to the scottish delegation.
10. This month greco-roman art will be shown in a cincinnati museum.
11. Shall we go to the mexican restaurant or the thai one?
12. The United States imports arab oil and mexican oil.
13. Mahatma Gandhi helped the indian people become free of british rule.
14. I prefer new england clam chowder over manhattan clam chowder.
15. We ate polish sausages at the carnival.

CHAPTER 21 Capitalizing Proper Adjectives

EXERCISE Choose which proper adjectives require capitalization.

_____ 1. My grandmother has a secret recipe for swedish meatballs.
 A Grandmother
 B Swedish Meatballs
 C Swedish

_____ 2. Maria likes only two types of music: rap music and turkish music.
 A Rap Music, Turkish Music
 B Rap, Turkish
 C Turkish

_____ 3. My friend Pierre is a francophile; he likes all things french.
 A French
 B Francophile, French
 C Francophile

_____ 4. The television broadcast the senate hearings.
 A Senate
 B Senate Hearings
 C Television, Senate

_____ 5. Do they sell idaho potatoes at the farmer's market?
 A Idaho
 B Idaho, Market
 C Idaho Potatoes, Farmer's Market

_____ 6. We are leaving early to avoid friday-afternoon rush hour.
 A Friday-Afternoon
 B Friday
 C Friday, Rush Hour

_____ 7. Every August the city fills with european tourists.
 A City, European
 B European
 C European Tourists

_____ 8. I am learning to play spanish folk music on the classical guitar.
 A Spanish Folk Music
 B Spanish, Classical
 C Spanish

_____ 9. Brett gets all his political ideas from the sunday newspaper.
 A Political
 B Sunday Newspaper
 C Sunday

_____ 10. The english language has adopted words from foreign languages.
 A English
 B English Language
 C English Language, Foreign Languages

_____ 11. This nineteenth century statue was sculpted from italian marble.
 A Century, Italian
 B Italian
 C Century, Italian Marble

_____ 12. These pretzels come from the dutch region of Pennsylvania.
 A Dutch Region
 B Region
 C Dutch

_____ 13. Nina is covering a political meeting for the republican newsletter.
 A Political, Meeting
 B Political, Republican
 C Republican

_____ 14. Many japanese cars are actually built in american-owned factories.
 A Japanese, American
 B Japanese Cars, American
 C Japanese, American-Owned

CHAPTER 21 Capitalizing Titles

[21D] Capitalize the titles of persons and works of art.

> **EXERCISE** Write the word(s) that should be capitalized in the blanks; if the sentence is correct, write C.

_____ 1. Why did your aunt Betsy send you a present?

_____ 2. My uncle has always lived on a farm.

_____ 3. Our new doctor lives in your neighborhood.

_____ 4. Tell me, senator, what do you think your chances for reelection are?

_____ 5. The president gave his State of the Union message before a joint session of Congress.

_____ 6. May I use the car this weekend, dad?

_____ 7. My dad always walks the dog after supper.

_____ 8. The Rotary Club will have a luncheon for senator-elect Jackson.

_____ 9. Have you ever heard uncle Max play the trumpet?

_____ 10. Please make an appointment with dr. Rodino to have your teeth cleaned.

_____ 11. Grover Cleveland was the last president to keep a cow at the White House.

_____ 12. One famous horsewoman is princess Anne.

_____ 13. Does your uncle Samuel live around here any more?

_____ 14. The most famous Southerner during the Civil War was general Robert E. Lee.

_____ 15. The chief justice spoke to a group of senators.

_____ 16. Can I make a right turn on a red light, officer?

_____ 17. Janice will be late to the meeting because she is at the dentist's office.

_____ 18. The poet Edna St. Vincent Millay won the Pulitzer Prize in 1923.

Name _____ Date _____

CHAPTER 21 — Capitalizing Titles

EXERCISE A Choose the answer that contains the correct form of capitalization of titles.

_____ 1. **A** Oscar Wilde wrote the play *The Importance of Being Earnest*.
  B Oscar Wilde wrote the play *the Importance of Being Earnest*.

_____ 2. **A** Rachel Carson, a marine biologist, wrote *Silent spring* in 1962.
  B Rachel Carson, a marine biologist, wrote *Silent Spring* in 1962.

_____ 3. **A** On May 13 and 15, we will perform *The Man who Came to Dinner*.
  B On May 13 and 15, we will perform *The Man Who Came to Dinner*.

_____ 4. **A** Shakespeare's *Romeo And Juliet* is a play about teenage romance.
  B Shakespeare's *Romeo and Juliet* is a play about teenage romance.

_____ 5. **A** A copy of the *Ladies' Home journal* was among the magazines in Dr. Hudson's waiting room.
  B A copy of the *Ladies' Home Journal* was among the magazines in Dr. Hudson's waiting room.

_____ 6. **A** Do you know who wrote the poem "To a mockingbird"?
  B Do you know who wrote the poem "To a Mockingbird"?

_____ 7. **A** Agatha Christie wrote *The Murder of Roger Ackroyd*.
  B Agatha Christie wrote *The murder of Roger Ackroyd*.

_____ 8. **A** Have you read the article "Why the City of Love is Cool and Gray"?
  B Have you read the article "Why the City of Love Is Cool and Gray"?

_____ 9. **A** During the Humphrey Bogart festival, we saw the film *The Maltese falcon*.
  B During the Humphrey Bogart festival, we saw the film *The Maltese Falcon*.

_____ 10. **A** We saw a revival of Gershwin's *Porgy and Bess* on Broadway.
  B We saw a revival of Gershwin's *Porgy And Bess* on Broadway.

EXERCISE B Complete each sentence with an appropriate title, capitalized correctly.

11. The last book that I read is _____

12. My favorite poem is _____

13. If I had a personal theme song, it would be _____

14. I never miss an episode of the television series _____

15. If I wrote a blog post about my day today, it would be called _____
_____

16. If I go see a movie this weekend, it will be _____

116 Grade 11 • Chapter 21: Capital Letters

CHAPTER 21   Capitalization Review

EXERCISE A In the following passage, decide which word(s) should be capitalized in each underlined part.

Yellowstone is the first national Park in the State. You should also see the historic national monument, devil's tower. According to a legend of the Sioux, this natural wonder was formed to help three girls escape from angry Rocky Mountain Grizzly bears. More recently, Wyoming was the setting of the film *Close encounters of the third Kind*.

_____ 1. **A** first National Park in the state
    B First National Park in the State
    C first national park in the State
    D first national park in the state

_____ 2. **A** historic National monument, devil's tower.
    B historic National monument, Devil's Tower.
    C historic national monument, Devil's Tower.
    D No error

_____ 3. **A** Sioux, this Natural Wonder
    B sioux, this natural wonder
    C sioux, this Natural wonder
    D No error

_____ 4. **A** Rocky Mountain grizzly bears
    B Rocky mountain Grizzly bears
    C Rocky Mountain Grizzly Bears
    D No error

_____ 5. **A** *Close Encounters of the third Kind*
    B *close encounters of the third kind*
    C *Close Encounters of the Third Kind*
    D No error

EXERCISE B Rewrite the following paragraph on the lines below, correcting any errors in capitalization.

During the American revolutionary war, Virginia played a leading role. In fact, at the 1775 Virginia convention, political Leader Patrick Henry cried out his famous words, "Give me Liberty, or give me death!" Mount Vernon, the first president's home, is also located in Virginia. Later at the end of the Civil war, general Robert e. Lee surrendered to Ulysses S. Grant at Appomattox, Virginia.

_____
_____
_____
_____
_____

Name _____ Date _____

CHAPTER 22 End Marks

[22A.1] A **declarative sentence** makes a statement or expresses an opinion and ends with a **period**. (.)
[22A.2] An **imperative sentence** gives a direction, makes a request, or gives a command. It ends with either a period or an **exclamation point**. (. or !)
[22A.3] An **interrogative sentence** asks a question and ends with a **question mark**. (?)
[22A.4] An **exclamatory sentence** expresses strong feeling or emotion and ends with an **exclamation point**. (!)

EXERCISE A Choose the appropriate end mark to each sentence: a period, question mark, or exclamation point. In the blank, label the sentence as declarative (D), imperative (IM), interrogative (IN), or exclamatory (E).

_____ 1. Do you have any valuable old bottles in your cellar _____

_____ 2. The United States began minting coins in 1792 _____

_____ 3. Is Cuba ninety miles south of Key West _____

_____ 4. I absolutely love this ice cream _____

_____ 5. Two Poles who served in the Continental Army became heroes _____

_____ 6. Run for your life _____

_____ 7. Did many Portuguese Americans emigrate from the Azores _____

_____ 8. Puerto Rico is not one of the fifty states _____

_____ 9. May I please have your ticket stubs _____

_____ 10. Show up for soccer practice by three o'clock _____

_____ 11. Have you ever played Monopoly _____

_____ 12. Trish, will you go to the square dance with me _____

_____ 13. Come down off that ladder right now _____

_____ 14. Will you please stop constantly tapping your foot _____

_____ 15. Come and have some cake with us _____

EXERCISE B Read the passage and then add a period, a question mark, or an exclamation point to each blank.

How much do you know about legendary pitcher Satchel Paige **(16)** _____ The Baseball Hall of Fame in Cooperstown, New York, inducted Satchel Paige in 1971 **(17)** _____ For his talent, his energy, and his showmanship, Paige became the most famous of the Negro Baseball League players **(18)** _____ If you want to know more about the great Satchel Paige, read *Maybe I'll Pitch Forever*, his autobiography **(19)** _____ If you want to visit the Hall of Fame, hurry **(20)** _____ The exhibition curators are lending a large number of the player's photographs and other mementos to a Canadian museum **(21)** _____

Name _____ Date _____

CHAPTER 22 Periods with Abbreviations

[22A.5] Use a period after most abbreviations. A dictionary can help you find the exceptions, which include some organizations and companies.

EXERCISE A Choose the correct form of the abbreviation in each sentence. Remember, not all abbreviations require periods.

_____ 1. United Nations
   A UN
   B U.N.

_____ 2. cash on delivery
   A COD
   B C.O.D.

_____ 3. Boulevard
   A Blvd
   B Blvd.

_____ 4. intelligence quotient
   A IQ
   B I.Q.

_____ 5. kilometer
   A km
   B km.

_____ 6. United Kingdom
   A UK
   B U.K.

_____ 7. North Dakota
   A ND
   B N.D.

_____ 8. pound
   A lb
   B lb.

_____ 9. Avenue
   A Ave
   B Ave.

_____ 10. January
   A Jan
   B Jan.

EXERCISE B Choose the sentence that is punctuated correctly.

_____ 11. A The plane is due about 5:00 pm.
       B The plane is due about 5:00 p.m.

_____ 12. A Anglo-Saxon rulers were buried in boats as early as 800 B.C..
       B Anglo-Saxon rulers were buried in boats as early as 800 B.C.

_____ 13. A The case against RM Lowry was established by the F.B.I.
       B The case against R. M. Lowry was established by the FBI.

_____ 14. A When Abe worked on the Panama Canal, he missed his favorite TV programs.
       B When Abe worked on the Panama Canal, he missed his favorite T.V. programs.

_____ 15. A Is our new principal's name Robert Noble, Jr.?
       B Is our new principal's name Robert Noble, Jr?

_____ 16. A The latest arrival was Arnoldo E. Okenga, Sr., M.D.
       B The latest arrival was Arnoldo E Okenga, Sr., MD.

Name _____ Date _____

CHAPTER 22 Commas That Separate

[22B.1] Use commas to separate items in a series.
[22B.2] In certain situations, use a comma sometimes to separate two adjectives that directly precede a noun and that are not joined by a conjunction.

EXERCISE Choose the sentence that is punctuated correctly.

_____ 1. **A** Chickadees, sparrows, and blue jays come to our bird feeder.
B Chickadees sparrows and blue jays come to our bird feeder.

_____ 2. **A** Hush puppies, chicken and dumplings, and black-eyed peas are Southern specialties.
B Hush puppies, chicken and dumplings and black-eyed peas are Southern specialties.

_____ 3. **A** Stars sparkle brighter on crisp, winter nights.
B Stars sparkle brighter on crisp winter nights.

_____ 4. **A** Drive carefully past schools behind buses and in parking lots.
B Drive carefully past schools, behind buses, and in parking lots.

_____ 5. **A** Pumpkins and corn and potatoes are native to the Americas.
B Pumpkins, and corn, and potatoes are native to the Americas.

_____ 6. **A** In our garden we have maroon, orange, pink, and white zinnias.
B In our garden we have maroon, orange, pink, and white, zinnias.

_____ 7. **A** We all turned out to welcome our exhausted victorious team.
B We all turned out to welcome our exhausted, victorious team.

_____ 8. **A** Bridal Veil, Vernal, and Yosemite Falls are all in Yosemite Park.
B Bridal Veil, Vernal, and Yosemite Falls, are all in Yosemite Park.

_____ 9. **A** The hottest, driest desert in the United States is Death Valley.
B The hottest driest desert in the United States is Death Valley.

_____ 10. **A** Sally has learned to be extra careful when she starts the car when she backs up and when she passes another car.
B Sally has learned to be extra careful when she starts the car, when she backs up, and when she passes another car.

_____ 11. **A** Hong Kong consists of Hong Kong, Kowloon, and the New Territories.
B Hong Kong consists of Hong Kong, Kowloon, and, the New Territories.

_____ 12. **A** No one can resist the puppy's sad brown eyes.
B No one can resist the puppy's sad, brown eyes.

_____ 13. **A** After visiting the museum, we walked through the park, ate at a café, and rode the trolley.
B After visiting the museum, we walked through the park ate at a café and rode the trolley.

_____ 14. **A** Would you rather go to the movies, the bowling alley, or, the carnival for your birthday?
B Would you rather go to the movies, the bowling alley, or the carnival for your birthday?

_____ 15. **A** Be careful under the hot bright sun: wear sunscreen.
B Be careful under the hot, bright sun: wear sunscreen.

Name _____ Date _____

CHAPTER 22 — Commas That Separate

EXERCISE A Write C if a sentence is correct. Write I if commas are used incorrectly and change the sentence so it is correct.

_____ 1. The robot Alpha picked up seven bolts and dropped them quickly carefully, and correctly into seven holes in the engine.

_____ 2. Alpha's pincers duplicate the movements of the human shoulder, arm, wrist, and fingers.

_____ 3. This robot lacks the charm of toy household and science-fiction robots.

_____ 4. It cannot do housework, walk, or lift, huge loads.

_____ 5. This inexpensive, easily made, model is widely used by car manufacturers.

_____ 6. Robots like Alpha are used in the United States, Europe, and Japan.

_____ 7. Some robots can carry weights use tools and reach for objects.

_____ 8. For simple routine jobs on assembly lines, Alpha is perfect.

_____ 9. A properly programmed Alpha does its job precisely, neatly, and alone.

_____ 10. Most robots, however, cannot distinguish between parts, adjust to new situations, or, make decisions.

EXERCISE B Write sentences that follow the directions below. Use commas where needed.

11. Include a series of verbs that describes the actions of an energetic kitten.
    _____
    _____

12. Include a series of nouns naming objects bought at a pet store.
    _____
    _____

13. Include a series of phrases describing where you searched for a lost hamster.
    _____
    _____

14. Include before a noun two adjectives that are separated by a comma.
    _____
    _____

15. Include before a noun two adjectives that are not separated by a comma.
    _____
    _____

CHAPTER 22 Commas in Compound Sentences

[22B.3] Use a comma to separate the independent clauses of a compound sentence if the clauses are joined by a coordinating conjunction.

EXERCISE Choose the sentence that is punctuated correctly.

____ 1. **A** Some people like kumquats, but I have never tasted one.
     B Some people like kumquats but I have never tasted one.

____ 2. **A** Ellen handed over the alarm clock, and I set it for 5:00 a.m.
     B Ellen handed over the alarm clock and I set it for 5:00 a.m.

____ 3. **A** I waved, and she waved back.
     B I waved and she, waved back.

____ 4. **A** Hedgehogs look like porcupines, but they are related to moles.
     B Hedgehogs look like porcupines but they are related to moles.

____ 5. **A** The Nile River used to flood Egypt annually, and fertilize the soil.
     B The Nile River used to flood Egypt annually and fertilize the soil.

____ 6. **A** I took a bite of the kiwi, for I was very curious.
     B I took a bite of the kiwi for I was very curious.

____ 7. **A** Hopi Indians are famous for their pottery and blankets, and they are also known as skillful weavers and carvers.
     B Hopi Indians are famous for their pottery and blankets and they are also known as skillful weavers and carvers.

____ 8. **A** Rivers are beautiful, yet they can be destructive.
     B Rivers are beautiful yet they can be destructive.

____ 9. **A** Surfers may go to Waikiki, or they can try the less-frequented beaches on Maui.
     B Surfers may go to Waikiki or they can try the less-frequented beaches on Maui.

____ 10. **A** The ostrich is the largest living bird, but it cannot fly.
     B The ostrich is the largest living bird but it cannot fly.

____ 11. **A** Commercial fishermen mostly fish with nets, but on the Grand Banks, they fish with lines and hooks.
     B Commercial fishermen mostly fish with nets but on the Grand Banks, they fish with lines and hooks.

____ 12. **A** Most aerial fireworks explode into trails of sparks, and then make loud booms.
     B Most aerial fireworks explode into trails of sparks and then make loud booms.

____ 13. **A** Some forest fires are caused by lightning, but many are started by careless humans.
     B Some forest fires are caused by lightning but many are started by careless humans.

____ 14. **A** Many Finnish people like to take hot saunas, and then jump into ice-cold pools.
     B Many Finnish people like to take hot saunas and then jump into ice-cold pools.

Name	Date

CHAPTER 22 Commas in Compound Sentences

EXERCISE A Insert a comma between the independent clauses of the following compound sentences if they are joined by a coordinating conjunction. If the sentence is correct, write *No Change*.

1. Now that spring has arrived the flowers are in bloom and the trees are budding.
2. I ran for the bus but I missed it when I slipped and fell into the puddle.
3. Joanna took the exam and felt confident.
4. I wake up first yet there is never enough hot water for the shower.
5. The dance is next Friday but I will be away.
6. Shereen loves chocolate but hates ice cream.
7. The decision was made quickly and behind closed doors.
8. Maddy refused the position for she is overqualified.
9. The radio was loud but no one complained.
10. The game was canceled and rescheduled for next Saturday.

EXERCISE B Edit the following passage, adding commas where needed and crossing out those that are incorrectly placed.

"Hors d'oeuvre" may be hard to spell but these bite-sized portions of food are usually not at all hard to make. All you need are some crackers and you've got the main ingredients for many popular hors d'oeuvres. Place something tasty—a small piece of cheese, a shrimp, or a slice of cucumber—atop your "base" and, sprinkle it with one of your favorite herbs. Voila! You've created an elegant snack for your guests or you have a delicious one for yourself. Egg rolls, crab puffs, and mini-quiches are also popular choices and, your guests will eat them up. Delicious hors d'oeuvres do not need to be fancy nor do they need to be expensive. Finger sandwiches make excellent party hors d'oeuvres but, their preparation can be time-consuming. Cheese and onion nachos are also a good choice for party food for they are easily made and can be quickly heated in the microwave.

CHAPTER 22 Commas After Introductory Elements

[22B.4] Use a comma after certain introductory structures, such as introductory words, prepositional phrases, participial phrases, and adverbial clauses.

> **EXERCISE** The introductory element in each sentence below is underlined. Choose the answer that identifies the type of introductory element of each sentence. Notice that each introductory element is followed by a comma.

_____ 1. <u>During the past 400 years</u>, people have been creating more comfortable furniture.
  A introductory word
  B participial phrase
  C prepositional phrase
  D adverbial clause

_____ 2. <u>Fastening cushions on top of seats</u>, they made chairs easier to sit on.
  A introductory word
  B participial phrase
  C prepositional phrase
  D adverbial clause

_____ 3. <u>When people traveled</u>, they carried their clothing in large chests.
  A introductory word
  B participial phrase
  C prepositional phrase
  D adverbial clause

_____ 4. <u>After an Italian designer attached legs</u>, the chest became furniture.
  A introductory word
  B participial phrase
  C prepositional phrase
  D adverbial clause

_____ 5. <u>Thus</u>, the first chest of drawers was made.
  A introductory word
  B participial phrase
  C prepositional phrase
  D adverbial clause

_____ 6. <u>Adding arms, backs, and cushions to chests</u>, other designers created sofas.
  A introductory word
  B participial phrase
  C prepositional phrase
  D adverbial clause

_____ 7. <u>During the 1500s and 1600s</u>, explorers brought Chinese furniture to Europe.
  A introductory word
  B participial phrase
  C prepositional phrase
  D adverbial clause

_____ 8. <u>In addition to Chinese furniture</u>, Japanese furniture fascinated Europeans.
  A introductory word
  B participial phrase
  C prepositional phrase
  D adverbial clause

_____ 9. <u>When the wealthy saw Chinese porcelain</u>, they were entranced.
  A introductory word
  B participial phrase
  C prepositional phrase
  D adverbial clause

_____ 10. <u>For exhibiting their porcelain</u>, they had joiners make cupboards.
  A introductory word
  B participial phrase
  C prepositional phrase
  D adverbial clause

CHAPTER 22   Commas After Introductory Elements

EXERCISE Edit the following passage, inserting commas where necessary and crossing out those that are not needed.

In the early eighteenth century, certain craftsmen became famous. Combining Greek and Roman and Oriental styles, Thomas Chippendale created a style of his own. Also, Robert Adam and George Hepplewhite created unique styles. When wealthy American colonists furnished their homes, they imported English furniture. Besides Chippendale, Thomas Sheraton created popular desks and chairs. Using such native woods as cherry and chestnut, American artisans created beautiful desks and cabinets. Furnishing Mount Vernon, George Washington showed a taste for native woods.

CHAPTER 22: Commonly Used Commas

[22B.5] Use commas to separate the elements in dates and addresses.

[22B.6] Use a comma after the salutation of a friendly letter and after the closing of all letters.

[22B.7] Use commas to enclose nouns of direct address.

[22B.8] Use commas to enclose parenthetical expressions.

EXERCISE Rewrite the following letter on the lines below, correcting any mistakes in comma usage.

August 13 2010

1208 Main Street
Des Moines IA 50023

Dear Mr. Carter

    I would like to apply for a summer job with your company located at 7536 MLK Boulevard Des Moines Iowa. Mr. Carter I think that I am the best candidate for the job. I have worked at several part-time jobs since I moved to Iowa in December, 2006. Consequently I believe I could help your company grow and become even more successful than it is currently. I am ready and willing by the way to supply you with recommendations from my previous employers. I look forward to hearing from you.

Sincerely

Carlos Gonzales

CHAPTER 22 Commas with Appositives, Adjectives, Titles, and Degrees

[22B.10] Use commas to enclose most appositives and their modifiers, unless the appositive identifies a person or thing by telling which one. Adjectives, titles, and degrees in the appositive position are also set off by commas.

EXERCISE Choose the sentence that is punctuated correctly with commas.

_____ 1. A A European plane, the *Concorde*, initiated supersonic service.
　　　　B A European plane the *Concorde* initiated supersonic service.

_____ 2. A Tiger Woods a golf star began playing golf at the age of two.
　　　　B Tiger Woods, a golf star, began playing golf at the age of two.

_____ 3. A Soap, a relatively soft material, is ideal for carving.
　　　　B Soap a relatively soft material is ideal for carving.

_____ 4. A Airports, such as La Guardia and O'Hare, are extremely congested.
　　　　B Airports such as La Guardia and O'Hare are extremely congested.

_____ 5. A Scott Joplin, the famous jazz composer, played for large audiences.
　　　　B Scott Joplin the famous jazz composer played for large audiences.

_____ 6. A Ethan Allen, a native of Vermont, formed a group called the Green Mountain Boys.
　　　　B Ethan Allen a native of Vermont formed a group called the Green Mountain Boys.

_____ 7. A Captain Adele Parfait, USMC, will speak at our next assembly.
　　　　B Captain Adele Parfait USMC will speak at our next assembly.

_____ 8. A The snowflakes soft and big had been falling all day.
　　　　B The snowflakes, soft and big, had been falling all day.

_____ 9. A Franklin D. Roosevelt, the only person to be president for more than two terms, was born January 30, 1882.
　　　　B Franklin D. Roosevelt the only person to be president for more than two terms was born, January 30, 1882.

_____ 10. A An eighteen-ton bell, the largest ever tuned, hangs in the Riverside Church.
　　　　B An eighteen-ton bell the largest ever tuned, hangs in the Riverside Church.

_____ 11. A The name, Old Glory, was given to our flag by a sea captain.
　　　　B The name Old Glory was given to our flag by a sea captain.

_____ 12. A The battleship, *Intrepid*, sits in a New York harbor.
　　　　B The battleship *Intrepid* sits in a New York harbor.

_____ 13. A The novel, written by John Steinbeck, was made into a movie.
　　　　B The novel written by John Steinbeck was made into a movie.

_____ 14. A Jen, my cousin, works in the Seagrams Building.
　　　　B Jen my cousin works in the Seagrams Building.

_____ 15. A Maurice babysits for the Gordons the famous singing duo.
　　　　B Maurice babysits for the Gordons, the famous singing duo.

CHAPTER 22 Commas with Appositives, Adjectives, Titles, and Degrees

EXERCISE Write C if the sentence is punctuated correctly and I if it is punctuated incorrectly. Add or delete commas where necessary to make the sentence correct.

_____ 1. One of our great American leaders was Martin Luther King Jr.

_____ 2. *Dying Gladiator* a famous statue is in the Louvre museum in Paris.

_____ 3. Lindbergh's plane *The Spirit of St. Louis* is hanging in the National Air and Space Museum in Washington.

_____ 4. Mary Margaret McBride, an American broadcaster, pioneered the modern talk show.

_____ 5. Halley's Comet was named after Edmund Halley a British astronomer.

_____ 6. The mountain laurel, or calico bush, is the state flower of Pennsylvania.

_____ 7. Judo a method of personal combat without weapons is based on a knowledge of leverage.

_____ 8. Helen Keller a famous American became deaf and blind in her childhood.

_____ 9. Carl Sagan Ph.D. is a founder of the Planetary Society.

_____ 10. The famous composer, Scott Joplin, died in 1917.

_____ 11. *Aliens*, my favorite science-fiction movie, is showing at the Plaza Theater.

_____ 12. I will be graduating in the spring semester 2013.

_____ 13. Those coffee beans, grown in the mountains of Columbia are famous around the world.

_____ 14. Robert Benton Jr., is the vice president of City Limits a technology-based company.

_____ 15. The inventor Nikola Tesla was instrumental in the development of radio and the harnessing of electricity.

CHAPTER 22 — Commas with Nonessential Elements

[22B.10] Use commas to set off a **nonessential** or **nonrestrictive** participial phrase or clause.

EXERCISE Revise any comma errors in the following passage by adding or crossing out commas. Some sentences are correct.

(1) Cosmetics are preparations, used externally by people who desire to enhance their looks.

(2) Seven-thousand-year-old Egyptian tombs contain jars used for holding soothing salves. (3) Ancient people trying to keep their skin from wrinkling in the hot sun used perfumed oils. (4) Egyptian women blackened their eyelashes and upper eyelids with kohl which is a substance made from soot.

(5) This is a practice, that is still common in Egypt. (6) From statements, made in the Old Testament, it seems that some Jewish people adopted the use of cosmetics from the Egyptians. (7) The Egyptian queen Cleopatra who loved two Roman emperors was famous for her brightly painted face. (8) Roman women using chalk and white lead made their faces white. (9) The Romans, used bleaches and lotions with which their barber shops were well stocked. (10) Believing it kept their skin soft, some people bathed in milk. (11) The Crusaders brought cosmetics to Europe where they are still in use.

CHAPTER 22 End Marks and Commas Review

EXERCISE A Revise any comma errors in the following passage. Add commas where necessary and cross out any commas that are not needed.

From 1986, to 1990, Diana Golden monopolized the World Disabled Skiing Championships and she also blazed a trail for future disabled athletes. Her greatest victory at the time, however, was her 1988 Olympic gold medal in the giant slalom for disabled skiers which was a demonstration sport at the time. She went on to break down some of the barriers, that separated athletes with disabilities from others. Pioneers, like her, are critical role models for younger people who also have disabilities or other issues that prevent them from thinking of themselves as athletes.

EXERCISE B Punctuate the following paragraph, revising any comma errors or end marks as needed.

Besides enjoying international success Ernest Hemingway obviously had an impact on other authors because many imitated his style He received the Nobel Prize for Literature as well as the Pulitzer Prize both prestigious awards He was awarded the Pulitzer Prize based on the artistic merit of *The Old Man and the Sea* a short novel but obviously a masterpiece This story is about a heroic old fisherman who badly wants to catch a great fish Hemingway often created characters whom life had treated badly but who behaved with courage and stoicism both characteristics of his "code hero."

Name _____ Date _____

CHAPTER 23 — The Possessive Form of Nouns

[23A.1] Add 's to form the possessive of a singular noun.
[23A.2] Add only an apostrophe to form the possessive of a plural noun that ends in *s*.
[23A.3] If a plural noun does not end in *s*, add 's to form the possessive, just as you would to a singular noun that does not end in *s*.

EXERCISE Choose the correct possessive form for each phrase.

_____ 1. the homework for this week
    A this weeks homework
    B this week's homework
    C homework's week
    D homeworks weeks

_____ 2. the handle of the basket
    A the basket's handle
    B the handle's basket
    C the baskets handle
    D the baskets' handle

_____ 3. the collars belonging to the cats
    A the cat's collars
    B the collar's cats
    C the cats' collars
    D the cats's collars

_____ 4. the value of the money
    A the monies value
    B the moneys value
    C the money's value
    D the moneys' value

_____ 5. the tusks of the walruses
    A the walruses' tusks
    B the walruses's tusks
    C the walruse's tusks
    D the tusk's walruses

_____ 6. the toys belonging to the children
    A the childrens' toys
    B the children's toys
    C the childrens's toys
    D the toys' children

_____ 7. the watch belonging to the lady
    A the ladies watch
    B the lady's watch
    C the ladie's watch
    D the ladys' watch

_____ 8. the speech given by the senator
    A the senator's speech
    B the speech's senator
    C the senators speech
    D the senators' speech

_____ 9. the plan of the thieves
    A the thieve's plan
    B the thieves's plan
    C the plan's thieves
    D the thieves' plan

_____ 10. the notebooks belonging to Janet
    A Janet's notebooks
    B Janets notebook's
    C Janets' notebooks
    D Janet notebooks'

_____ 11. the ears of a deer
    A a deers ears
    B a deers' ears
    C a deer's ears
    D a deers's ears

_____ 12. the tail of the fox
    A the foxes tail
    B the foxe's tail
    C the fox's tail
    D the foxs' tail

Name _____   Date _____

CHAPTER 23 The Possessive Form of Nouns

EXERCISE Write the correct form of the possessive for the underlined word.

_____ 1. With <u>Mr. Huang</u> assistance, we learned to paddle a canoe.

_____ 2. After two <u>weeks</u> vacation, we were happy to be home again.

_____ 3. <u>Becky</u> email told me all about her trip to Mexico.

_____ 4. My <u>father-in-law</u> motorcycle is his pride and joy.

_____ 5. Have you seen the <u>men</u> garden club exhibit in the mall?

_____ 6. Have you been invited to <u>Dan</u> birthday party?

_____ 7. I was not impressed with the much-touted <u>singer</u> debut album.

_____ 8. The <u>puppies</u> whining kept me up all night.

_____ 9. My <u>sister-in-law</u> house has just been painted brown.

_____ 10. On <u>Captain Davis</u> advice, we took the boat out of the water.

_____ 11. I just opened a savings account at the <u>First Federal Bank</u> Main Street office.

_____ 12. The <u>boys</u> chorus won first prize in the competition.

_____ 13. I put <u>Mary</u> scarf in the hall closet.

_____ 14. Even <u>*The New York Times*</u> editors occasionally make grammatical mistakes.

_____ 15. I bought this shirt on sale in the <u>women</u> department.

_____ 16. We found <u>Chris</u> ticket just before the bus arrived.

_____ 17. The <u>chairs</u> cushions were left in the rain.

_____ 18. <u>Thursday</u> meeting has been postponed until Friday.

Name _____ Date _____

CHAPTER 23 — The Possessive Form of Pronouns

[23A.4] The possessive forms of personal pronouns and the pronoun *who* do not use apostrophes.

EXERCISE Write the correct form of the possessive for the underlined word.

_____ 1. After the election <u>everyone</u> vote was carefully counted.

_____ 2. Don't tell me that beautiful new car is <u>your</u>.

_____ 3. <u>Somebody</u> costume is hanging on the back of a chair out front.

_____ 4. Their poster is better drawn than <u>our</u>.

_____ 5. <u>No one</u> grades have been posted on the bulletin board.

_____ 6. If these seats are ours, where are <u>their</u>?

_____ 7. The fact that we are so late is really <u>nobody</u> fault.

_____ 8. The horse was wearing a straw hat on <u>it</u> head.

_____ 9. Where the parade will end is <u>anybody</u> guess.

_____ 10. It's too late to exchange your name for <u>her</u>.

_____ 11. The cat hid <u>it</u> kittens under the stairs.

_____ 12. <u>Everyone</u> homework should be handed in by noon.

_____ 13. No debate team is better than <u>our</u>.

_____ 14. The class ring found under my desk is <u>your</u>.

_____ 15. The one with the blue stripes on it is <u>her</u>.

CHAPTER 23: The Possessive Form of Pronouns

EXERCISE Write the correct possessive form for each phrase.

_____ 1. the phone belonging to me

_____ 2. the books belonging to him

_____ 3. the car belonging to them

_____ 4. the picture that you took

_____ 5. the team belonging to them

_____ 6. a garden belonging to anyone

_____ 7. a place for everybody

_____ 8. the batteries belonging to it

_____ 9. the jacket belonging to me

_____ 10. the newspaper belonging to someone

_____ 11. the proposal given by them

_____ 12. the scene acted by us

_____ 13. the flowers belonging to everyone

_____ 14. the fan belonging to him

_____ 15. the program prepared by her

_____ 16. the award belonging to me

_____ 17. the leash belonging to it

_____ 18. the notes taken by them

_____ 19. the trophy won by us

_____ 20. the supplies belonging to you

CHAPTER 23 Apostrophes and Joint Ownership

[23A.6] Add 's to only the last word to show joint ownership.
[23A.7] Add 's to each word to show separate ownership.

> **EXERCISE** Choose the type of ownership shown by the underlined words in each sentence. Write S for separate and J for joint.

_____ 1. We will perform Gilbert and Sullivan's operetta *The Mikado*.

_____ 2. Phil and Brett's dog won a blue ribbon at the dog show.

_____ 3. Lucy's and DaShawn's entries in the ceramic contest won prizes.

_____ 4. Both Asheville's and Brevard's newspapers are delivered here daily.

_____ 5. Painting that backdrop was Neal and Jasper's project.

_____ 6. This winter Bill's and Cindy's cars have been in for repairs again.

_____ 7. Our performance of Lerner and Lowe's *My Fair Lady* was a hit.

_____ 8. What will be Paul's and your authority for all spelling disputes?

_____ 9. Alaska's and Siberia's land masses were once joined.

_____ 10. Melanie's and Hugo's gardens each have tomatoes, corn, and green beans.

_____ 11. Where are Sean's and Annie's sunglasses?

_____ 12. Tim Rice's and Elton John's musical talents are well documented.

_____ 13. I like Agatha Christie's and Elizabeth George's murder mysteries.

_____ 14. Ella Fitzgerald's and Otis Redding's songs are among my favorites.

_____ 15. My brother's and sister's allowances are always carefully spent.

Name _____ Date _____

CHAPTER 23 Other Uses of Apostrophes

[23A.9] Use an apostrophe in a contraction to show where one or more letters have been omitted.
[23A.8] Add *'s* to form the plural of lowercase letters, some capital letters, and some words used as words.

> **EXERCISE** Choose the word needing an apostrophe or an apostrophe and an *s*. If the sentence is correct, choose *No error*.

_____ 1. Are those all As on your report card?
  A A's
  B your's
  C No error

_____ 2. Why havent you dotted your j's?
  A haven't
  B j's'
  C No error

_____ 3. Ounce for ounce, humans aren't as strong as most insects.
  A human's
  B insects'
  C No error

_____ 4. Why dont you put on your pajamas and go to bed?
  A don't
  B pajamas'
  C No error

_____ 5. Your capital Bs look funny.
  A B's
  B your's
  C No error

_____ 6. I've decided to attend the local community college after high school.
  A high's
  B community's
  C No error

_____ 7. Isnt anyone's picture on a one-dollar bill?
  A Isn't
  B one-dollar's
  C No error

_____ 8. Can you write your 7s more clearly?
  A you's
  B 7's
  C No error

_____ 9. Thats the only inhabited island on the river.
  A That's
  B inhabited's
  C No error

_____ 10. No insect exists that doesnt have three pairs of legs.
  A doesn't
  B pairs'
  C No error

_____ 11. The sun warms the part of Earth that its shining on.
  A warm's
  B it's
  C No error

_____ 12. This cactus hasnt bloomed in five years.
  A hasn't
  B year's
  C No error

_____ 13. When you write your paper, don't use so many *his*s.
  A *his*'es
  B *his*'s
  C No error

_____ 14. Im sure he'll be right back with his tools.
  A I'm
  B his'
  C No error

_____ 15. The race starts at five oclock.
  A start's
  B o'clock
  C No error

CHAPTER 23 — Semicolons Between Clauses; with Transitional Words

[23B.1] Use a semicolon between closely related clauses of a compound sentence when they are not joined by a conjunction.

[23B.2] Use a semicolon between clauses in a compound sentence that are joined by certain conjunctive adverbs or transitional words.

> **EXERCISE** Choose the answer that correctly uses a semicolon or a semicolon and a comma. If the sentence is correct, choose *No error*.

____ 1. Most insects have a highly developed sense of smell however most humans do not.
- **A** Most insects have a highly developed sense of smell; however, most humans do not.
- **B** Most insects have a highly developed sense of smell, however; most humans do not.
- **C** No error

____ 2. The river was very wide nevertheless we crossed it without difficulty.
- **A** The river was; very wide nevertheless, we crossed it without difficulty.
- **B** The river was very wide; nevertheless, we crossed it without difficulty.
- **C** No error

____ 3. I went outside she went inside.
- **A** I went outside; she went, inside.
- **B** I went outside; she went inside.
- **C** No error

____ 4. Black pepper is the whole fruit; white pepper is made by removing the outer hull.
- **A** Black pepper is the whole fruit white pepper; is made by removing the outer hull.
- **B** Black pepper, is the whole fruit; white pepper is made by removing the outer hull.
- **C** No error

____ 5. The hill wasn't very steep in fact it was rather flat.
- **A** The hill wasn't, very steep in fact; it was rather flat.
- **B** The hill wasn't very steep; in fact, it was rather flat.
- **C** No error

____ 6. I like to grow plants consequently I own a lot of gardening tools.
- **A** I like to grow plants, consequently; I own a lot of gardening tools.
- **B** I like to grow plants; consequently, I own a lot of gardening tools.
- **C** No error

____ 7. Lime juice was once considered necessary to avoid scurvy however vitamin C from any other source is just as effective.
- **A** Lime juice was once considered necessary to avoid scurvy; however, vitamin C from any other source is just as effective.
- **B** Lime juice was once considered, necessary to avoid scurvy; however vitamin C from any other source is just as effective.
- **C** No error

____ 8. I have an atlas; my brother uses it to study geography.
- **A** I have an atlas; my brother uses it, to study geography.
- **B** I have an atlas, my brother uses it; to study geography.
- **C** No error

CHAPTER 23 Semicolons to Avoid Confusion

[23B.3] Use a semicolon instead of a comma in certain situations to avoid confusion.

> **EXERCISE** Write C on the line if the semicolon usage is correct. If the sentence is incorrect, revise the sentence, using semicolons and commas correctly.

1. Our exams will be given on Sunday, April 1; Sunday, April 8; and Saturday, April 14.

2. The first team is Ann, Lewis, and Chen, and the second team is Conner, Oleg, and Kim.

3. Our plane landed in Chicago, Illinois, Denver, Colorado, and Los Angeles, California.

4. My grandmother visited last week on Wednesday; Thursday; and Friday.

5. The children wrote to their relatives in New York City; Albany; and Rochester.

6. My brothers live in Boise, Idaho; Costa Mesa, California; and Jackson, Mississippi.

7. Dodo birds and saber-toothed tigers are extinct; and manatees are endangered.

8. We still have not received votes from Seattle, Washington, Portland, Oregon, or Helena, Montana.

Name _____ Date _____

CHAPTER 23 Colons

[23B.5] Use a colon before most lists of items, especially when a list comes after an expression such as *the following*.

[23B.6] Use a colon between independent clauses when the second clause explains or restates the first.

> **EXERCISE** Write C on the line if the colon usage is correct. If the sentence is incorrect, revise the sentence, using colons correctly.

1. There are generally two causes of smog: burning fuel and exhaust emissions from automobiles.

2. Megan received A's in three subjects biology, history, and trigonometry.

3. The plane from Honolulu is scheduled to land at 1:130 a.m.

4. The following are three kinds of oranges Seville, mandarin, and navel.

5. Christopher's favorite: foods include the following pizza, hamburgers, and steak.

6. I typically enjoy two types of movies: psychological thrillers and romantic comedies.

7. Margie always sets her alarm for 700 a.m.

8. We grow the following kinds: of apples Fuji, Delicious, and Golden Delicious.

CHAPTER 23 Italics (Underlining)

[23C.2] Italicize (underline) the titles of long written or musical works that are published as a single unit. Also italicize (underline) the titles of paintings and sculptures and the names of vehicles.

EXERCISE Underline each letter, number, word, or group of words that should be italicized.

1. On Sunday mornings we often watch <u>Face the Nation</u> on TV.

2. What does <u>muchacha</u> mean in Spanish?

3. How many <u>4</u>s are there in a dozen?

4. I recently read Chekov's <u>The Cherry Orchard</u>.

5. The <u>Orient Express</u> is a train made famous by Agatha Christie.

6. The word <u>brioche</u> is French for a kind of bread.

7. <u>Old Ironsides</u> is still afloat in Boston Harbor.

8. My favorite work of Shakespeare's is <u>Hamlet</u>.

9. The summer theater is performing <u>Arsenic and Old Lace</u>.

10. I always read the classifieds in <u>The New York Times</u>.

11. <u>Crouching Tiger, Hidden Dragon</u> is an innovative and beautiful film.

12. Last month's <u>National Geographic</u> includes an article on the Appalachian Mountains.

13. Sting's <u>Brand New Day</u> is my latest album purchase.

14. How many flights into space has the <u>Columbia</u> made?

15. Dr. Smith suggested I see the movie <u>Big</u>.

16. How many <u>6</u>s are in this column?

17. What does the Latin term <u>id est</u> mean?

18. Fran told me how to spell <u>committee</u>.

19. I've seen the Broadway musical <u>Rent</u> four times.

20. This month's <u>Consumer Reports</u> compares laptop computers.

CHAPTER 23 Quotation Marks with Titles

[23D.1] Use quotation marks to enclose the titles of chapters, articles, essays, stories, one-act plays, short poems, songs, episodes from a TV series, and movements from a musical composition.

EXERCISE Add quotation marks where needed.

1. Dr. Thomas's essay "Speaking of Speaking" was in *Discover*.

2. "The Rising Sun" was my favorite chapter.

3. The short poem "More Music" appears in this magazine.

4. Blake's composition "The Road to Mexico" was fascinating to read.

5. The article on the front page of the paper declared "Heat Soars, Breaking Record."

6. Bruce Springsteen sang "Born in the U.S.A." at the concert last week.

7. Judy Troy's short story "In One Place" was very funny.

8. My one-act play is entitled "The Silver Mice."

9. I like Aretha Franklin's version of the song "Respect."

10. I can't get the song "Vida La Vida" out of my head.

11. The book *The Time Traveler's Wife* was recently made into a movie.

12. Please read the chapter "Standard Conversions" for tomorrow's class.

13. The article "The Heart of Wall Street" made me want to visit the New York Stock Exchange.

14. Do you know all the verses of "American Pie"?

15. "Self-Reliance" is an essay by Ralph Waldo Emerson.

Name _____ Date _____

CHAPTER 23 Direct Quotations

[23D.2] Use quotation marks to enclose a person's exact words.
[23D.3] Begin each sentence of a direct quotation with a capital letter.

EXERCISE A If quotation marks are used correctly, write C. If they are missing or incorrect, make the appropriate changes to the sentence.

_____ 1. "If you stop to be kind, said Mary Webb, you must swerve often from your path."

_____ 2. "The only thing you have to fear," said Franklin D. Roosevelt, "is fear itself."

_____ 3. Frances Havergal said, "Sorrow which is never spoken is the heaviest load to bear."

_____ 4. The saying If you think education is expensive, try ignorance is attributed to Derek Bok.

_____ 5. "The best way to keep one's word is not to give it, declared Napoleon.

_____ 6. If all the world were just, there would be no need for courage, said Plutarch.

_____ 7. Samuel Johnson said, "Praise, like gold," owes its value only to its scarcity.

_____ 8. T. S. Eliot explained, "Immature poets imitate; mature poets steal."

_____ 9. "Even if you're on the right track," warned Will Rogers, you'll get run over if you just sit there."

_____ 10. "There is always room for beauty, advised Florence Coates."

EXERCISE B Rewrite each sentence using correct capitalization.

11. "Great is truth. Fire cannot burn, nor water drown it," Wrote Alexandre Dumas.

12. Mathew Green wrote, "laugh and be well."

13. According to Mary Poole, "he who laughs, lasts."

14. "A signature reveals a man's character—and sometimes even his name," Said Evan Esar.

15. "A man's feet should be planted in his country," said George Santayana, "But his eyes should survey the world."

16. A German expression states, "all or nothing!"

CHAPTER 23 — Commas and End Marks with Direct Quotations

[23D.4] Use a comma to separate a direct quotation from a speaker tag. Place the comma inside the closing quotation marks.

[23D.5] Place a period inside the closing quotation marks when the end of the quotation comes at the end of a sentence.

[23D.6] Place the question mark or the exclamation point *outside* the closing quotation marks when the sentence itself is a question or an exclamation.

EXERCISE A Write C in the blank if a sentence is punctuated correctly. Write I if the sentence is punctuated incorrectly and make the appropriate changes, crossing out or adding commas.

_____ 1. "I don't make jokes" wrote Will Rogers. "I just watch the government and report the facts."

_____ 2. "Better watch out!" yelled Jenny. "The light just turned red."

_____ 3. "I'll slow down" said the driver "but stop shouting at me."

_____ 4. "If people don't want to come out to the ball park," said Yogi Berra "nobody's going to stop them."

_____ 5. "I read all of these books by myself", said my little sister proudly.

_____ 6. "I really liked *Harriet the Spy* when I was your age," I said.

_____ 7. Robert Byrne said "Science has not yet found a cure for the pun."

_____ 8. "Tell your brother it's time for dinner," said my father, "and go wash your hands."

_____ 9. "Turn off the television," I called out, "It's time to eat."

_____ 10. "People who never get carried away should be" wrote Malcolm Forbes.

EXERCISE B Write C in the blank if a sentence is punctuated correctly. Write I if the sentence is punctuated incorrectly and make the appropriate changes crossing out or adding end marks.

_____ 11. Who said, "Life is but a dream?"

_____ 12. "Let me play the game"! my younger brother protested.

_____ 13. My mother asked, "How was your chemistry test?"

_____ 14. "You missed the turn!" Phyllis yelled from the backseat.

_____ 15. Did Peter say, "I don't like chocolate chip cookies?"

_____ 16. I asked my teacher, "When will we review the material for the math test?"

_____ 17. Gary said, "This tree was planted a hundred years ago".

_____ 18. "Are you researching the Civil War for your history paper"? Mr. Benson asked.

_____ 19. Monte asked, "Did the radio broadcast say that the storm may cause a power failure?"

_____ 20. Working at the computer, Victoria shouted, "I just lost ten pages of my final draft"!

CHAPTER 23 Hyphens

[23E.2] Use a hyphen when writing out the numbers **twenty-one** through **ninety-nine**.
[23E.3] Use one or more hyphens to separate the parts of some compound nouns and adjectives. Also use one or more hyphens between words that make up a compound adjective in front of a noun.
[23E.4] Use a hyphen after the prefixes *ex-*, *self-*, and *all-* and before the suffix *-elect*. Also use a hyphen with all prefixes before a proper noun or a proper adjective.

EXERCISE Choose whether the sentence has a word that needs to be hyphenated or contains no error as written.

_____ 1. Is your mother self employed?
    A self-employed
    B No error

_____ 2. Your essay was very well written.
    A well-written
    B No error

_____ 3. The recipe called for one third of a cup of blueberries.
    A one-third
    B No error

_____ 4. There are twenty two days left until the opening of the art gallery.
    A twenty-two
    B No error

_____ 5. That computer program is no longer up to date.
    A up-to-date
    B No error

_____ 6. My cereal bowl is only one third full.
    A one-third
    B No error

_____ 7. Is your sister in law coming with us to the store?
    A sister-in-law
    B No error

_____ 8. To become an attorney at law, you must first pass a tough examination.
    A attorney-at-law
    B No error

_____ 9. David collects half dollar coins.
    A half-dollar
    B No error

_____ 10. One quarter of the student body was out with the flu.
    A One-quarter
    B No error

_____ 11. Frank hit the bull's-eye ninety nine times out of a hundred.
    A ninety-nine
    B No error

_____ 12. He answered only three quarters of the questions.
    A three-quarters
    B No error

_____ 13. A mid December snow is common.
    A mid-December
    B No error

_____ 14. My cousin Antonia is always off in a world of make believe.
    A make-believe
    B No error

_____ 15. I was nervous about confronting him face to face.
    A face-to-face
    B No error

Name _____ Date _____

CHAPTER 23 Dashes and Parentheses

[23E.6] Use dashes (—) to set off an abrupt change in thought.
[23E.7] Use dashes to set off a parenthetical expression or an appositive that includes commas. Also use dashes to call special attention to a phrase.
[23E.8] Use dashes to set off a phrase or a clause that summarizes or emphasizes what has preceded it.
[23E.9] Use parentheses (()) to enclose information that is not related closely to the meaning in the sentence.

EXERCISE Choose the answer that uses dashes or parentheses correctly.

_____ 1. A mako that is, a mackerel shark can be dangerous.
  A A mako—that is, a mackerel shark—can be dangerous.
  B A mako (that is, a mackerel shark) can be dangerous.

_____ 2. The boys all of them laughing ran through the field barefoot.
  A The boys (all of them laughing) ran through the field barefoot.
  B The boys—all of them laughing—ran through the field barefoot.

_____ 3. Moles, mice, and voles all rodents have been spotted there.
  A Moles, mice, and voles—all rodents—have been spotted there.
  B Moles, mice, and voles (all rodents) have been spotted there.

_____ 4. My foot hurts see the place with the bruise?
  A My foot hurts—see the place with the bruise?
  B My foot hurts (see the place with the bruise)?

_____ 5. Ben Franklin statesman, diplomat, inventor was also an author.
  A Ben Franklin—statesman, diplomat, inventor—was also an author.
  B Ben Franklin (statesman, diplomat, inventor) was also an author.

_____ 6. Several students ten in all missed the trip to the planetarium.
  A Several students—ten in all—missed the trip to the planetarium.
  B Several students (ten in all) missed the trip to the planetarium.

_____ 7. Franklin D. Roosevelt was elected to four terms as president 1932–1945.
  A Franklin D. Roosevelt was elected to four terms as president—1932–1945.
  B Franklin D. Roosevelt was elected to four terms as president (1932–1945).

_____ 8. Many games for example, chess and checkers are played by computers.
  A Many games (for example, chess and checkers) are played by computers.
  B Many games—for example, chess and checkers—are played by computers.

_____ 9. Onions, carrots, and potatoes all were added to the stew.
  A Onions, carrots, and potatoes (all were added to the stew).
  B Onions, carrots, and potatoes—all were added to the stew.

_____ 10. Many people even Harvard graduates have mistaken ideas about the reason for the earth's seasons.
  A Many people—even Harvard graduates—have mistaken ideas about the reason for the earth's seasons.
  B Many people (even Harvard graduates) have mistaken ideas about the reason for the earth's seasons.

CHAPTER 23 Other Punctuation Review

EXERCISE Correct the following paragraphs by crossing out and/or adding correct punctuation or capital letters.

A number of gifted writers for instance, Edgar Allan Poe, John Keats, and Sylvia Plath are famous for having died young, as well as other things. All three of the writers works contained dark themes especially Poe and Plath: all three writers found early fame.

In 1833, the young Poe submitted The Message Found in a Bottle to a Baltimore newspaper The Saturday Visitor and won $50; his first notable payment. Many well read people praised Poes work, but others were alarmed by his macabre themes. Decades later, James Whitcomb Riley the Indiana Poet Laureate would pass off one of his own poems as written by Poe. It was considered a great hoax: literary publications gave it a great deal of coverage. Poes distinctive style was almost an invitation to parody and imitation.

Arthur Conan Doyle whose work is still read today modeled his most famous character on a real person. A literary scholar named Forster wrote: I believe that Dr. Joseph Bell was Conan Doyle's model for Sherlock Holmes." Several biographical facts of Bells life for example, his uncanny ability to deduce information from small clues are evident in the character of Holmes. Doyle's Sherlock Holmes was the first popular sleuth in this genre. Doyle tried to stop writing about Holmes his most successful creation by introducing other characters in other titles. It was no use the public wanted more of Holmes. Arthur Conan Doyle was eventually knighted by King Edward VII for his proBritish accounts of the Boer War.

Name _____ Date _____

CHAPTER 24   Spelling Patterns

[24A.1] When you spell words with *ie* or *ei*, *i* comes before *e* except when the letters follow *c* or when they stand for the sound long *a*.

[24A.2] Words that end with a syllable that sounds like "seed" are usually spelled with *-cede*.

> **EXERCISE** Choose the word in each group that is spelled correctly. Use a dictionary if you need help.

_____ 1. **A** excedingly
          B exceedingly
          C exsedingly

_____ 2. **A** feirce
          B feerce
          C fierce

_____ 3. **A** riemburse
          B reimburse
          C re-imburse

_____ 4. **A** overweieght
          B overwieght
          C overweight

_____ 5. **A** niegh
          B neiegh
          C neigh

_____ 6. **A** ceiling
          B cieling
          C celing

_____ 7. **A** soverign
          B soveriegn
          C sovereign

_____ 8. **A** superceeding
          B superseding
          C superceding

_____ 9. **A** preesthood
          B preisthood
          C priesthood

_____ 10. **A** neighborly
          B nieghborly
          C neghborly

_____ 11. **A** spiceiest
          B spiciest
          C spiceist

_____ 12. **A** accedes
          B acsedes
          C acceeds

_____ 13. **A** reenterpret
          B rienterpret
          C reinterpret

_____ 14. **A** aweigh
          B awegh
          C awiegh

_____ 15. **A** unyilding
          B unyeilding
          C unyielding

_____ 16. **A** socieity
          B society
          C soceity

_____ 17. **A** conseder
          B conceeder
          C conceder

_____ 18. **A** deities
          B dieties
          C deieties

Name _____ Date _____

CHAPTER 24 Spelling Patterns

EXERCISE A Write C if the underlined word in each sentence is spelled correctly. If it is spelled incorrectly, write the correctly spelled word in the blank.

_____ 1. Scot was alarmed to see how much his hairline was <u>receeding</u>.

_____ 2. We took a trip to Finland, where it is "mandatory" for tourists to visit a <u>riendeer</u> herd.

_____ 3. <u>Piety</u> is not one of the more widely practiced virtues in the twenty-first century.

_____ 4. If you have a <u>greevance</u>, take it up with the customer service desk, please.

_____ 5. <u>Sceintific</u> knowledge is increasing exponentially, in part thanks to the facility of computers.

_____ 6. If he becomes a <u>luitenant</u> in the army, he'd better learn how to spell his own title.

_____ 7. <u>Cheifly</u>, he doesn't want anyone to think they can get away with it.

_____ 8. Are you as proud of your <u>achievement</u> as I am?

_____ 9. The <u>anteciedent</u> to a pronoun is a noun.

_____ 10. That is the most <u>inefficieint</u> use of time you could imagine.

EXERCISE B Underline any misspelled words and write the correct spelling on the blank. If all words are spelled correctly, write C on the blank.

_____ 11. Professor Smith is insufficeiently concerned with students using their cell phones to cheat.

_____ 12. The infeilder is likely to raise eyebrows, come time for the team photograph.

_____ 13. Let me interceed, so you won't lose any sleep over this.

_____ 14. It's inefficeint to run an air conditioner on high all day and then turn it off completely at night.

_____ 15. Look! There's a medieval castle halfway up the mountain.

_____ 16. Make sure you bring sufficient water to the tennis courts.

Name _____   Date _____

CHAPTER 24 Plurals

EXERCISE Identify the incorrect plural form in each group of words, numbers, or symbols. Use a dictionary if necessary.

_____ 1. A strawberries
          B cherreys
          C blueberries

_____ 2. A hoaxs
          B axes
          C boxes

_____ 3. A volcanoes
          B patioes
          C cameos

_____ 4. A ellipses
          B algae
          C bacteriums

_____ 5. A Japaneses
          B French
          C British

_____ 6. A daughter-in-laws
          B mothers-in-law
          C fathers-in-law

_____ 7. A #s
          B @'s
          C &s

_____ 8. A oboes
          B pianoes
          C piccolos

_____ 9. A inquirys
          B dairies
          C studies

_____ 10. A bookshelves
          B eyeteeth
          C firemans

_____ 11. A 1930s
          B 1920's
          C 1760s

_____ 12. A bushes
          B crashs
          C radishes

_____ 13. A lunches
          B benches
          C stitchs

_____ 14. A midwifes
          B headscarves
          C jackknives

_____ 15. A formulas
          B indexes
          C parenthesises

Name _____ Date _____

CHAPTER 24 Plurals

EXERCISE A Write the plural form of each of these nouns.

1. monkey _____

2. lily of the valley _____

3. crisis _____

4. window _____

5. U _____

6. suffix _____

7. attorney general _____

8. tray _____

9. runner-up _____

10. staff _____

11. stereo _____

12. holiday _____

13. breadwinner _____

14. sauce _____

15. tomato _____

EXERCISE B Underline and correct any misspelled words in each sentence.

16. The 1980's were a time of economic excess. _____

17. Her replys were so rude that I felt attacked. _____

18. The scenarioes were all tragic; none of them seemed to offer any hope at all. _____

19. The datas were out-of-date and—even worse—had been plagiarized. _____

20. The reindeers on his wall are cute, but suggest a certain immaturity. _____

150   Grade 11 • Chapter 24: Spelling

Name _____ Date _____

CHAPTER 24 Spelling Numbers

[24C.1] Spell out numbers that can be written in one or two words. Use numerals for other numbers. Always spell out a number that begins a sentence.

[24C.2] Always spell out numbers used to tell the order.

[24C.3] Use a numeral for a date when you include the name of the month. Always use numerals for the year.

EXERCISE A Choose the sentence that is written correctly.

_____ 1. **A** It is estimated that there are more than 6,800,000 camels in Somalia.
B It is estimated that there are more than six million eight hundred thousand camels in Somalia.

_____ 2. **A** Yesterday was the 1st time I had seen the film *The Sound of Music*.
B Yesterday was the first time I had seen the film *The Sound of Music*.

_____ 3. **A** Michael owns 125 red marbles, 102 blue marbles, and 16 green marbles.
B Michael owns 125 red marbles, 102 blue marbles, and sixteen green marbles.

_____ 4. **A** Our physics class was held in Room 101 on the first floor.
B Our physics class was held in Room One Hundred One on the first floor.

_____ 5. **A** 6 families are living in Sam's apartment building.
B Six families are living in Sam's apartment building.

_____ 6. **A** At an auction Elvis Presley's driver's license was sold for seven thousand, four hundred dollars.
B At an auction Elvis Presley's driver's license was sold for $7,400.

_____ 7. **A** 98 percent of the students in our class have passed the test.
B Ninety-eight percent of the students in our class have passed the test.

EXERCISE B If the sentence is correct, write C on the line. If the sentence is incorrect, rewrite it so it is correct.

8. There are 5 people waiting to have their photos taken.

_____

9. Lukas earns 5 dollars an hour on weekdays and 8 dollars an hour on weekends.

_____

10. Our zip code is easy to remember, because it is two zero two zero two.

_____

11. 101 people have donated their time to the charity.

_____

12. The film *Nashville* was released in nineteen seventy-five.

_____

Name _____   Date _____

CHAPTER 24 — Prefixes and Suffixes

[24D] A **prefix** is one or more syllables placed in front of a base word to form a new word. A **suffix** is one or more syllables placed after a base word to change its part of speech and possibly also its meaning.
[24D.1] When you add a **prefix**, the spelling of the base word does not change.
[24D.2] Most of the time when adding a **suffix**, simply affix it to the end of the word.

> **EXERCISE** Choose the word in each group of three words that is misspelled. Use a dictionary if necessary.

_____ 1. A iciest
        B evenness
        C permited

_____ 2. A colicy
        B gracious
        C perilous

_____ 3. A reexamine
        B imutable
        C dissolution

_____ 4. A moralize
        B vigorrous
        C uniquely

_____ 5. A nauseous
        B miscellaneous
        C contageous

_____ 6. A antequarian
        B intervene
        C insubordination

_____ 7. A unnoticed
        B dissatisfied
        C disimilarity

_____ 8. A elimination
        B servicable
        C extinguish

_____ 9. A plagiarist
        B shily
        C uneasiness

_____ 10. A overide
        B monopolize
        C biannual

Name _____ Date _____

CHAPTER 24   Prefixes and Suffixes

EXERCISE A Underline and correct any misspelled words in each sentence.

_____ 1. His pitching isn't helped by the fact that he's overthrowwing.

_____ 2. My connivving roommate has been eating my food and lying about it.

_____ 3. Removal of the canccerous growth usually spells success for the patient.

_____ 4. This is the hazziest day of the golf tournament.

_____ 5. A missanthrope is generally someone who can do without other human beings.

_____ 6. The transsition between high school and college is a tough one: high school graduates are neither children nor quite adults.

_____ 7. Margaret Atwood is one of my favorite novellists.

_____ 8. Her novels are unargueably well-written.

_____ 9. The dog isn't ready yet; they're just latherring him up now.

_____ 10. His chuminess didn't convince me of his sincerity.

EXERCISE B Add the prefix or suffix to each of these base words and write the new word.

11. frosty + ness _____

12. journey + s _____

13. memory + able _____

14. judge + ment _____

15. possess + ion _____

16. decent + cy _____

17. study + ous _____

18. exert + ion _____

19. guilty + est _____

20. dissolve + ing _____

Name _____ Date _____

CHAPTER 24 Spelling Review

EXERCISE In the paragraph below, some of the underlined words are spelled incorrectly. Write the correct form of the word on the lines below. If the word is spelled correctly, write C on the line.

    (1) <u>1st</u>, of all the stringed **(2)** <u>instruments</u>, the violin is the most **(3)** <u>versatile</u>. It is **(4)** <u>unnusual</u> to see violas and **(5)** <u>celloes</u> in a country music group, and you will **(6)** <u>rareily</u> see **(7)** <u>banjoes</u> and guitars in the symphony orchestra. Violins, however, have dual **(8)** <u>lifes</u>. Going by the name of "fiddles," they do **(9)** <u>themselfs</u> proud, playing with folk or bluegrass **(10)** <u>comboes</u>. As violins, they are the **(11)** <u>principal</u> voices in symphonies, sonatas, and **(12)** <u>concertoes</u>. Alone, they can play **(13)** <u>soloes</u>. With a cello and a viola, they can play trios. **(14)** <u>Actualy</u>, they are almost as versatile and popular as **(15)** <u>pianoes</u>, and they are much more portable!

1. _____
2. _____
3. _____
4. _____
5. _____
6. _____
7. _____
8. _____
9. _____
10. _____
11. _____
12. _____
13. _____
14. _____
15. _____

Name	Date

APPENDIX Power Rules

[RULE 1] Use only one negative form for a single negative idea.
[RULE 9] Use the contraction *'ve* (not *of*) when the correct word is *have*, or use the full word *have*. Use *supposed* instead of *suppose* and *used* instead of *use* when appropriate.
[RULE 10] For sound-alikes and certain words that sound almost alike, choose the word with your intended meaning.

> **EXERCISE** The following letter contains errors. For each underlined word or phrase, correct the error on the lines below.

Dear Jorge:

It's **(1)** not hardly believable that I am writing to ask you a favor already. I hope **(2)** its a good time for you to **(3)** here about this. I **(4)** would of written you sooner, but this summer has just been **(5)** to crazy. I **(6)** use to think summers were fun, but **(7)** not no more. After I turned sixteen, my parents made me work. Speaking of work, do you know anything about the Internships Abroad program? I'd especially like to go to Mexico, so I could improve my Spanish. I'm **(8)** suppose to do one of these things to make my application for colleges look better. I **(9)** should of warned you about this earlier, so you **(10)** could of asked your father about this. Does he have any contacts in Monterey? **(11)** I wouldn't of never asked you to do this if I wasn't desperate. But there **(12)** isn't nothing I'd like better than to see you and your family (especially your sister Zoilita). Please send me an e-mail or visit my Facebook page, so I can get a **(13)** cents of what you think my chances are.

Cheers,
Conor Burke-Smith

1. _____
2. _____
3. _____
4. _____
5. _____
6. _____
7. _____
8. _____
9. _____
10. _____
11. _____
12. _____
13. _____

APPENDIX: Power Rules

[RULE 2] Use mainstream past tense forms of regular and irregular verbs.
[RULE 3] Use verbs that agree with the subject.
[RULE 6] Use a consistent verb tense except when a change is clearly necessary.

EXERCISE The following article contains errors. For each underlined word or phrase, correct the error on the lines below.

Members of the Ames High School Environmental Club **(1)** come together for its first meeting of the fall semester on August 25. New students **(2)** brang lots of ideas and enthusiasm to their first get-together. Club president Navid Emami announced that there **(3)** was eight new students joining the club this year. "They really **(4)** wants to push the city of Ames to go green." The meeting got down to business with a summary of past actions. New member Bridgit Killackey asked if the group **(5)** does a clean-up of Skunk Creek last year. Emami responded, "Everyone **(6)** think that was the most awful mess we'd ever seen. Broken washing machines, bicycles, you-name-it—people dumped all kinds of things in that poor creek." Some members of the group groaned, remembering what a tough chore the creek clean-up **(7)** were. A senior club member reported on a conference he'd **(8)** be to over the summer. Nationally, he said, groups like theirs **(9)** was growing in number and visibility. Before they adjourned, the club members **(10)** draw up a list of possible actions for them to pursue during the school year.

1. _____
2. _____
3. _____
4. _____
5. _____
6. _____
7. _____
8. _____
9. _____
10. _____

APPENDIX Power Rules

[RULE 4] Use subject forms of pronouns in subject position. Use object forms of pronouns in object position.
[RULE 5] Use standard ways to make nouns possessive.

> **EXERCISE** The following letter contains errors. For each underlined word, correct the error on the lines below.

Dear Mayor Culver:

   (1) Me and my little brother Scot would like to ask that the city reconsider **(2)** you plan to build a bike path to the new mall. **(3)** Us two would like to see you use the **(4)** citys' money in better ways. Given the terrible economy, it seems unlikely that this bike path is going to benefit the majority of **(5)** we citizens. **(6)** Me and Scot, who ride our bikes a lot, would never use a path that went parallel to a major freeway. Talk about dangerous! Yet, that is the **(7)** councils's plan. If it were up to **(8)** he and I, this particular bike path would be nixed. **(9)** Him and my plan would be for existing bicycle paths to be hooked together better than they are right now. **(10)** Us young people would probably use our bikes a lot more if the paths were better connected. **(11)** Lincoln Streets' bike path is a good example of one that doesn't connect to any others. My dad and **(12)** me talk about these kinds of things a lot—**(13)** him's in construction engineering. I thought you might like to know **(14)** he and my opinion. **(15)** Scots, too!

Thank you for your attention.

Sincerely,

Shota Hattori

1. _____
2. _____
3. _____
4. _____
5. _____
6. _____
7. _____
8. _____
9. _____
10. _____
11. _____
12. _____
13. _____
14. _____
15. _____

APPENDIX Power Rules

[RULE 7] Use sentence fragments only the way professional writers do, after the sentence they refer to and usually to emphasize a point. Fix all sentence fragments that occur before the sentence they refer to and ones that occur in the middle of a sentence.

[RULE 8] Use the best conjunction and/or use punctuation for the meaning when connecting two sentences. Revise run-on sentences.

EXERCISE The following article contains sentence fragments and run-on sentences. Correct each error on the lines below. Be sure to use proper punctuation.

(1) Over the last few years. (2) Sales of juvenile and young adult novels have grown. (3) Much of this growth can be attributed to the popularity of the Harry Potter novels. (4) The first Harry Potter book, *Harry Potter and the Sorcerer's Stone,* was published in 1997, it was an instant hit with children and grown-ups alike. (5) Readers around the world were introduced to Harry Potter, an orphan, and Hermione and Ron. (6) Who are his best friends at the Hogwarts School of Witchcraft and Wizardry. (7) Potter is a loyal friend, skilled wizard. (8) And reluctant archenemy of the wicked Voldemort. (9) Many fantasy books have become modern classics. (10) Including the *Narnia* and *Lord of the Rings* series. (11) That were written by C.S. Lewis and J.R.R. Tolkien, respectively. (12) However, none has been such a worldwide phenomenon as the Harry Potter series. (13) Which has been read by hundreds of millions and turned into seven blockbuster motion pictures. Harry Potter has charmed many a young person into becoming a lifelong reader.

1. Combine sentences 1 and 2. _____

2. Revise sentence 4. _____

3. Revise sentences 5 and 6. _____

4. Combine sentences 7 and 8. _____

5. Combine sentences 9, 10, and 11. _____

6. Combine sentences 12 and 13. _____

Name _____   Date _____

APPENDIX Power Rules Review

EXERCISE The following article contains errors. For each underlined word or phrase, correct the error on the lines below.

Even though you don't have a **(1)** dog. The new Mattapoisett public dog park is a must-see destination. Parks and Recreation members Tony Smith and Rebecca McBurney **(2)** is inviting everyone in town to visit the ten-acre hangout for resident canines. According to Smith, **(3)** "Me and Rebecca have been behind this project one hundred percent, but some of the city council members **(4)** was skeptical." He laughed. "You **(5)** haven't seen nothing until you've seen little tiny Chihuahuas running and playing alongside great big German **(6)** shepherds. And having a blast!" McBurney smiled. "We **(7)** should of warned everyone how much fun it was going to be to visit this **(8)** park, you can enjoy yourselves even if you **(9)** doesn't own dogs." McBurney **(10)** suppose the idea for a dog park came from a citizens' **(11)** task force. That was formed to discuss lifestyle improvements for Mattapoisett. Both commissioners admit to a special fondness for dogs, however. **(12)** "I use to have five dogs at one time," Smith said, chuckling. "I really **(13)** could of use this park back then." The **(14)** citizen's new dog park will have a free grand opening on **(15)** June 4, after that users will be charged a small fee.

1. _____
2. _____
3. _____
4. _____
5. _____
6. _____
7. _____
8. _____
9. _____
10. _____
11. _____
12. _____
13. _____
14. _____
15. _____

NOTES